GEORGE WASHINGTON ATE HERE!

A frolic through history with food and famous folks!

GEORGE WASHINGTON ATE HERE!

A frolic through history with food and famous folks!

BY T. UPTON RAMSEY

Edited by Don Ware

The best recipes from 12 years of food columns orginally published in **The Salt Lake Tribune**

Library of Congress Catalog Card Number: 97-90689

ISBN: 0-9658000-0-8

Cover Design and Layout: Ingenious, Steve McRea
Typesetting: Accu-Type Pre Press, Paula Conway
18th Century Woodcut Illustrations: Bowles & Carver, New York, New York
Printed by Publishers Press, Salt Lake City, Utah

First Printing, 1997

Printed in U.S.A.

Bill of Fare

ACKNOWLEDGMENTS FROM UPPY

Over the more than 50 years that I have been trying hundreds, probably thousands, of recipes (as a student of food preparation, as a professional chef, as a "kitchen cook" for my family, friends and my own students) I have had the opportunity to read and research every source I could find on the subject of food. I have read every cookbook I have bought, every book Rhoda has found and brought to me or that has been given to me by friends or students, and—of course—most food magazines. Thus, I've developed so many sources from which to draw, so many volumes to rely on, so much material to assimilate and translate and work on and even make changes in, it would take another book simply to acknowledge my reference sources. In going through my library, I reviewed some of the books from which I have "borrowed" most liberally, and they are listed below.

However, there is no way I can list every source (my mind is simply not that nimble any more). I would like to thank the editors of and contributors to *Gourmet, Food and Wine,* and *Bon Appetit*—magazines which I find particularly appealing and informative.

The historical information, the facts and anecdotes dealing with various foods, peoples, or periods of history and time, have been much more difficult to compile. But, fun to find, nonetheless. My major in history whetted my appetite even further. Making it even more fun and rewarding, were the very helpful people in the Marriott Library at the University of Utah who have given me such helpful guidance.

I hope you share with me the pleasure of cooking and the enjoyment of knowing a little bit more about the foods we prepare and enjoy.

There are so many sources I would like to list, so many people I would like to acknowledge, so much to say—so little space. If you are among those I have omitted, please forgive me—it was unintentional. I owe so much to so many and I am forever grateful.

A very incomplete list of my sources:

Henry Haller—*The White House Family Cookbook*, Random House, 1989.

Waverley Roat—*Food*, Simon & Schuster, 1980.

William Harlen Hale—*Horizon Cookbook*, American Heritage, 1968.

American Heritage Cookbook by the editors of American Heritage Magazine, 1964.

Poppy Cannon—*The President's Cookbook*, Funk and Wagnalls, 1968.

Robert Carrier—*Food, Wine and Friends*, Sidgwick & Jackson, 1980.

Mary Randolf—*The Virginia Housewife*, John Plaskitte, 1836.

Margaret C. Tyme—*Housekeeping in Old Virginia*, Louisville, Kentucky, 1890.

Acknowledgments (cont.)

Oscar Tschirhy—*Oscar of the Waldorf*, Sall Field, 1896.

The First Ladies Cookbook, GMG Publishing, 1982.

Steven Raichlen—*A Celebration of Seasons*, Poseidon Press, 1988.

F. Point—*MA Gastronomi*, Lyceum Books, 1974.

Reay Tannahill—*Food in History*, Stan and Day, 1973

Faye Levy—*Lavarenne Tour Book*, Peanut Butter Publishing, 1980.

Harold McGee—*The Curious Cook*, North Point Press, 1980.

Raymond Sokolov—*The Saucier's Apprentice*, Alfred A. Knopf, 1976.

Raymond Oliver—*La Cuisine*, Tudor Publishing, 1967.

Helen Bullock—*Williamsburg Art of Cookery*, Dietz Press, 1938.

Elizabeth Miller—*Sarah Daft Home Cook Book*, Inland Printing, 1923.

Kansas State College—*Practical Cooking*, Kansas State Printing, 1939.

Derin Adair—*The Original White House Cookbook*, Saalfield Press, 1983.

Henri-Paul Pellagrat—*Modern French Culinary Art*, World Publishing Co., 1966.

FOREWORD . . . BY DON WARE

Have you ever met any one who actually read a foreword in a book? Neither have we. So, how could we get some one to read this one? Solution: ask some of Uppy's students and former students (he teaches cooking classes three nights a week in three separate sessions—men only "women cry when things go awry" he says—) to make a contribution. This way, there will be at least 16 readers of *this* foreword, since we have 16 contributors.

The usual cooking class routine is for students (maximum of eight per class) to begin arriving about 6 p.m. (You grab an apron—proudly monogrammed "USC", not for the university but for "Uppy's School of Cooking"), then you find the evening's menu and recipes and select which item or items you would prefer to prepare. We usually pair off into two students per menu item and prepare it laboriously, asking Uppy dozens of very elementary questions ("How do you chop an onion?") which he takes in stride and, with a great deal of patience, answers for the umpteenth time.

I remember his initial advice (which he delivers to every beginning class): "The first thing you do when you enter the kitchen is fill the sink with soapy water; as you finish with each dish, bowl, plate or utensil, put it in the water. When you're waiting for something to happen—like the water to boil—wash as many dishes as you have time for and set them aside to dry. When the meal is cooked, you'll have very few dishes left to overwhelm you."

His second matter of advice: "Read the *entire* recipe before you start preparing it." Excellent advice, I was to later learn.

I was making the salad dressing one night, and the recipe called for a cup of red wine, which I dutifully added. The next line read "vinegar." Red wine vinegar is what I should have added. But the salad dressing was among the best the class had ever tasted, at least as far as we remember.

There is a waiting list to get into the classes—and with good reason. Even if we cooked nothing, it's such a wonderful experience to share in Uppy's charm and his sense of humor and his knowledge and wonderful patience with those of us who know little (or nothing) about cooking, and to enjoy the comradery that his magnetism creates.

And, if he really likes you, he'll let you watch "Jeopardy" with him while you're having a glass of wine or the beverage of your choice.

Here's what some other students think:

"In Uppy's classes, we have experienced WWII bombing raids over Africa, Italy and Europe, along with every wonderful cuisine you can imagine." (Uppy was a pilot during World War II and loves to talk about his incredible experiences).

—**Steve Lowe**
Restaurateur

FOREWORD . . .

"Three years of classes and I'm still here, still learning."

—Rob Elliott
Commercial Developer

"Uppy has put up with his stable of amateur cooks for years now, answering the same questions again and again, somewhat patiently. To emphasize the learning process, Uppy requires us to eat our failures as well as our successes. My fellow Monday niters feel that we are superior to the more staid Tuesday and Wednesday students. Our often questioned claim is that, since all three classes prepare the same meal each week, the Monday group has the task of fine tuning all the recipes. This, of course, requires a higher level of culinary expertise than that exhibited by those other people who take up the challenge on Tuesdays and Wednesdays. The real payoff for my Monday night struggles is not this self-imposed fame. It is that I can share with family and friends the many wonderful meals Uppy has allowed me to discover."

—Robert V. Sanders
Computer Technology Consultant
(Former owner, major snack food company)

"A veritable potpourri of the taste buds."

—Steve Sala
Banker

"An education in much more than cooking."

—Manoli Sargetakas
Fabric Distributor

"Uppy understands great food. Better yet, Uppy understands that great food is only a forum for fellowship. His classes not only nurture an appreciation for imaginative preparation—they make for a warm gathering of friends. And friendship is what Uppy does best."

—Mickey Gallivan
Advertising Executive

FOREWORD . . .

"His classes prove that passion is not limited to the bedroom."

—Clayton Barnes
Commercial Real Estate

"My favorite remembrance of the class was my surprise as a non-domestic male to find it such a truly infectious experience."

—John Ware
Insurance Executive

"Three full binders of recipes plus comradery of the evening—but cooking is the main force. Nine years of classes and looking forward to the next one."

—Alan Crandall, M.D.
Professor, Ophthalmology, University of Utah

"So much fun, I don't mind doing the dishes."

—Brent Maxfield
Certified Public Accountant

"An experience not limited to the palate."

—Kent Chard
Restaurateur

"That Uppy's recipes should appear in print is, in itself, a gift to all who love good food and the preparation that goes into it. Pity, though, those who have never partaken of a T. Upton class, for that is where one learns to cook, not just assemble the ingredients. And for that—we, those of us who have trundled in and out of his house all those years—are fortunate, for his tutelage, as well as friendship. Nevertheless, as Uppy says, 'eat up, before it gets cold.'"

—Charlie Seldin
Graduate, T. Upton Ramsey's Les Petit Cor de la Cuisine Francaise

FOREWORD . . .

"Now with the publication of GEORGE WASHINGTON ATE HERE, others may join those of us who have been fortunate enough to be students of Chef Ramsey and share cooking under the tutelage of this remarkable man. Cooking T. Upton's way as found in these pages is a must for anyone who cooks and enjoys recipes seasoned with historical flavor."

—E. Barney Gesas
Attorney at Law

"The most memorable memory of Uppy's classes is arriving earlier than the other would-be cooks to look at the night's recipes taped to the front of the refrigerator. The first one there has first choice of menu items to prepare: salad, soup, meat, vegetables or dessert. I usually prefer the meat course as it gives me the opportunity to try things I'd never try otherwise— like Beef Wellington. In fact, I was so smug about this beef success, I even served it to my family in place of turkey for Thanksgiving!

—Duane Hill
Marketing Consultant

"The recipes are almost fool-proof. The food is only surpassed by the wonderful stories that abound in the classes."

—Bill Gibbons
Former CEO, Construction Company

*"We learn to slice, sauté and glaze,
We chop, we poach, to win his praise.
We boil, we braise, we blanch and taste.
We lift our cups and lift our glasses—
To Upton Ramsey's cooking classes."*

—Winter Horton
Public Relations Executive

BUT FIRST, A WORD FROM RHODA...

How lucky I am to have lived for over 45 years with a divine cook, historian, humorist, and "devoted dad." His antics and anecdotes in the kitchen have brought joy to thousands of readers in the many years his culinary column has appeared in 𝕿𝖍𝖊 𝕾𝖆𝖑𝖙 𝕷𝖆𝖐𝖊 𝕿𝖗𝖎𝖇𝖚𝖓𝖊.

My friends are always asking me and our children, Rochelle, Lisa and Tom what our favorite family recipes are? This is a hard question to answer because the king of our kitchen has rarely ever fixed anything that did not please our palates. The few times that he has had a failure we have reveled in it because it proves that even the best chefs are not always foolproof.

After much deliberation I would recommend to you:

Page 7   ROSE PETAL PRESERVES —
          Great to give to friends for Christmas.
Page 9   COL. RAMSEY'S APRICOT CHUTNEY —
          I can just eat it straight out of the jar by the spoonful. I love it with pork roast.
Page 34   BUCHANAN-LANE CHICKEN SALAD —
          Sometimes I add purple seedless grapes for color and taste.
Page 41   TERRIFIC TURKEY SOUP —
          Even if we were invited out for Thanksgiving, I would not go, for I would miss
          Uppy's turkey soup always made the Saturday after "Turkey Day."
Page 63   LEMON AND SAFFRON CHICKEN —
          A different version always pleasing to my taste buds.
Page 72   SPINACH STUFFED TURKEY MEAT LOAF —
          Great for me because it is fairly low in fat and calories.
Page 108 LOBSTER NEWBURG —
          We once served it to guests in our dining room and it ignited so
          ferociously the wall paper went up in flames!
Page 164 WINE JELLY MOLD —
          I like it best when he makes it with grape juice.
Page 169 APPLE CAKE — Great to take on a canyon picnic.

Now enough from me. Our sincere thanks to Don Ware, (former CEO of Harris and Love, Inc. Advertising). Without him we could never have made our "cook book dream" come true.

Enjoy!

Rhoda Ramsey

CHAPTER

Relishes

Apricot

Cranberries

Mushrooms

Pear

The Art of Artichokes

The artichoke was a native of Sicily—or possibly native to Carthage first, then transplanted on Carthaginian territory in Sicily. During the Middle Ages, Europeans did not seem to be eating artichokes, except in Sicily. The vegetable returned to Europe via Naples and progressed to Florence, where it was extensively cultivated in 1519.

This was 15 years before the birth of Catherine de Medici, yet she is commonly given credit for introducing it to France. This is a reasonable assumption, however, as she was a native of Tuscany where she grew up eating artichokes. When 14 years old, she married Henry II and moved to France. It was then considered scandalous for a maiden or young woman to eat a vegetable reputed to be an aphrodisiac. Thus she gave it notoriety by her scandalous fondness of it.

In early America, the artichoke was a rare and almost unknown luxury. The Spanish introduced it to California when they arrived. The French always listed it on the bill of fare when they held Louisiana. When the Spanish left California, it seems to have departed with them—only to return a century later.

California now produces the nation's entire commercial crop of artichokes, about 70 million pounds a year or about three-quarters of an artichoke per person. Other varieties of the vegetable are grown in the United States and in Europe, but the globe variety accounts for virtually the total production in California.

Even though it was considered a rare luxury in Martha Washington's day, she included it in her family recipes. Her recipe for a standard artichoke sauce is just as popular today as it was when she served it.

Martha Washington Artichoke Sauce

Artichokes
1 1/2 pounds butter
1/4 teaspoon nutmeg
Pepper to taste
1/2 cup flour
Juice of 1 lemon

In a pan over boiling water, melt 1/4 pound (1 stick) of the butter. Add nutmeg and pepper to taste. Stir in the flour and cook over simmering water for 15 to 20 minutes. Do not let it brown. Just before serving, add remaining butter (1 1/4 pounds); stir until melted. Add lemon juice. Serve hot with warm artichokes.

Artichoak

DOLLEY AND JEEMY

CHAPTER

1

Relishes

During the James Madison administration, parties at the White House during the holiday season were as grand as any ever held there.

When Dolley Madison hosted a party it was brilliant and dazzling. At dinner, Dolley presided, while James preferred to sit in a chair at the middle of the table, thus relieving him of having to serve their guests. On all social and domestic matters, "Jeemy" as she called him, deferred to his wife. It was customary for the hostess to serve and carve. She enjoyed this since she understood carving and knew where the best bits lay. James Madison, small and slender, was a sparing eater. Dolley, on the other hand, was plump, buxom and round, a connoisseur of good food. Considering the frequency of her entertaining, it's ironic that only a few of her choice recipes and favorites were recorded. It may be that they were lost in the White House fire of 1814.

Even though there was no official Thanksgiving Day during the Madison presidency, we do know that Dolley served roast turkey and cranberry relish during the holiday season. While she was in charge, the bills at the White House were high— sometimes as much as $50 a day. That $50 seems even higher when one learns that in that day a whole turkey cost only 75 cents. We have no record as to the cost of the cranberries for the relish used for these inexpensive White House turkeys.

DOLLEY MADISON CRANBERRY RELISH

3 oranges, thin skinned

1 cup uncooked cranberries, picked over

1 cup sugar, or to taste

Put the 3 small unpeeled oranges through the coarse blade of a meat grinder. (I use a processor.) Grind the cranberries in the same manner. Combine oranges and cranberries in a large bowl and mix in sugar to taste, keeping the flavor on the tart side. Cover the bowl and keep overnight in the refrigerator. Stir several times.

Orange Tree

THE ARTHUR ERA

Chester A. Arthur became president the night of Sept. 19, 1881, upon the death of James E. Garfield.

When the Garfield family vacated the White House, it was in need of renovation, and the new president insisted that redecorating and maintenance be done before he moved in. Sen. Jones offered his home on Capitol Hill for use as a temporary executive mansion so the president could supervise the renovation. In addition to the usual refinishing of walls and replacement of worn carpets, curtains and upholstery, additional furniture was ordered for the downstairs rooms. The president's upstairs study was decorated and new wood-burning fireplaces were included in every room. For the first time, an elevator was installed. The president ordered the accumulation of many administrations to be cleared from storerooms and sold at public auction.

The president's family consisted of his daughter and a teenage son. His wife Ellen died early in the year of his election. He persuaded his younger sister, Mary Arthur McElroy, to act as hostess for the executive mansion. She brought from Albany her two young daughters and a French governess.

Mrs. McElroy proved to be a tactful and gracious hostess. The president also brought a French chef from New York and his faithful family cook to staff the kitchen. President Arthur, an epicure, insisted on good food and drink for himself and his guests. His household orders from New York included fine wines, good cigars and gourmet foods. Official entertaining did not begin that first winter out of respect for the late president, but in March President Arthur initiated a series of elegant state dinners that established his reputation for hospitality.

When the Washington Monument was completed and formally presented to the United States March 2, 1885, the president gave an elegant banquet at the White House for a select group of guests. A condiment put up in the kitchens each year was a Mushroom Ketchup. It was served with most meat dishes at these very special dinners.

MUSHROOM KETCHUP

10 pounds mushrooms
1/2 cup salt
1 large onion, chopped
1 teaspoon ground allspice
1 teaspoon ground cloves
1 teaspoon prepared horseradish
Pinch of cayenne
1 cup cider vinegar

Wipe mushrooms with a cloth until clean. Chop mushrooms fine; mix with salt and let stand overnight. Next day, rinse mushrooms. To the pulp and juice, add chopped onions, allspice, cloves, horseradish, cayenne and vinegar. Heat until boiling and simmer until thickened, about 30 minutes, stirring occasionally. If desired, strain. If mixture is too thick, add more vinegar. Seal in hot sterilized jars. To ensure sealing, process in boiling water bath for 15 minutes.

Mushrooms

All About Peppers

Chapter

1

Relishes

Brightly colored and exotic, chilies and sweet peppers have come to be associated with many cooking traditions of the world. Although they belong to the same family, there is a world of difference between the fierce heat of the small chili and the mild spiciness of sweet peppers.

It was Columbus who brought the plants to Europe. He called them "peppers" because the heat of the chilies so closely resembled the spice he sought. The new flavoring was enthusiastically used in Europe. And within 100 years, the same enthusiasm had spread to Asia and Africa.

The sweet or bell pepper is a crisp vegetable, mildly sweet and spicy and eaten raw or cooked. The chili is used only as a flavoring but is eaten by some brave folk in competitions in Latin America and parts of the United States. Sweet ripe peppers are dried and ground to make the spice paprika, which is slightly peppery but not hot. Dried chilies are ground to make cayenne pepper and are combined with other spices to generate chili and curry powders and chili seasoning.

Sweet peppers are available in red, green and yellow — sometimes black. Chilies should be handled with care, in that they contain a pungent oil which can cause burning to the eyes, nose and throat. When cleaning them, wear rubber gloves. Do not touch your face while preparing chilies and always wash your hands well afterward.

Try the following recipe for a quick addition to your menu.

Red Pepper Sauce

This sauce is called Rouille because of its rust color. It goes well with any pasta and makes a good dip for vegetables.

1 large sweet red pepper, grilled, skinned, seeded, and chopped

1 small red chili, blanched, seeded, and chopped

1 clove garlic, minced

2 tablespoons fresh bread crumbs

4 tablespoons olive oil

2 to 3 tablespoons warm water

Salt and black pepper

Combine the sweet pepper, chili and garlic in a processor or mortar; puree to a smooth paste. Turn puree into a bowl and work bread crumbs into it. Gradually stir in olive oil. Slowly beat in warm water and season to taste.

A Rose Is A Rose

One blustery March day, I was in Boston at a cooking convention and met a chef and instructor named Steven Raichlen. Steven has published several cookbooks and owns and operates a mountain cooking school in New England in the summer and an island cooking school in the Caribbean in the winter. He shared this recipe for Rose Petal Preserves with me.

CHAPTER 1

Relishes

When roses are in full bloom lots of petals will fall off. This abundance of petals makes for a good time to try this recipe. Rose Petal Preserves makes a wonderful gift— and you can be pretty sure the recipient does not already own a jar. A perfect treat is in store for you when used as a filling for a tart or even on toast.

ROSE PETAL PRESERVES

2 quarts gently packed, clean, unsprayed
    rose petals
1 cup unsweetened apple juice
4 cups sugar
1/4 cup fresh lemon juice
2 strips lemon peel

Remove the bitter white heel from each of the petals. Place petals in a large non-aluminum saucepan and add 3 cups boiling water. Using a wooden spoon, gently push the rose petals down into water, bruising them to release their flavor. Cover the pan and let the petals steep for 20 or 30 minutes. Transfer the petals with a slotted spoon to a piece of cheesecloth and squeeze them back into the pan. Reserve petals.

Add the apple juice, sugar, lemon juice and lemon peel to the rose water and bring to a full boil. Reduce heat and simmer until liquid reaches 220 degrees on a jelly thermometer. Skim off froth and remove lemon peel.

Return the petals to sauce and stir gently to separate and distribute them evenly. When mixture returns to a jelly stage, remove from heat; ladle into hot, sterilized 1-cup jars. Wipe any drips from the edge of jars and seal with preserving lids. To ensure sealing, process in boiling water bath for 5 minutes. Turn jars upside down and check for leaks. Right them and let cool. Store in a cool, dry place. Makes six 1-cup jars. If used for filling tarts, use any standard tart dough recipe.

Rose

The Pristine Pear

Chapter 1

Relishes

Pears are a cook's ally. No other fruit can be bought hard and, within a few days of resting in your kitchen, become juicy, smooth and perfect for use. In Europe, there are more than 5,000 named varieties, and in America there are at least 1,000, though only a few reach the markets.

In America, we have more pears known as Williams and Bartletts, due to the fact that it was propagated by an English grower named Williams and introduced to America by an American, Bartlett. It has a sweet, musky flavor and a smooth skin that turns from dark green to yellow as it ripens. It is best to eat when its speckles are still surrounded by a tiny halo of green on the golden skin. These pears are bad travelers and should be eaten as soon as they are ripe.

Pears are ideal for cooking. You can poach them in wine or syrup or bake them like apples. They are wonderful when turned into a cake. I like them best when they are peeled and served with toasted walnuts and a fine bleu cheese.

When you have more pears than you know what to do with, pear chutney is your solution. Even those of you who have never bottled anything will be lured by this recipe.

Pear Chutney

1 1/2 cups cider vinegar

2 cups brown sugar, packed

3 1/2 pounds firm pears, peeled, cored, chopped

1 medium onion, chopped

1 cup golden raisins

1 1/2 tablespoons chopped fresh ginger

1 clove garlic, minced

1/2 teaspoon cayenne pepper

2 teaspoons salt

1/2 teaspoon cinnamon

1/2 teaspoon ground cloves

2 teaspoons mustard seeds

In a large kettle, bring the vinegar and sugar to a boil. Stir until the sugar is dissolved. Add pears, onion, raisins, ginger, garlic, cayenne, salt, cinnamon, cloves and mustard seeds. Bring to a boil. Reduce heat and simmer, uncovered, stirring occasionally. Chutney should be thick and will take at least 1 1/2 hours or longer to reach this consistency.

Pour into hot sterilized jars and wipe rims clean; seal. Process in boiling water for 10 minutes. Remove from water and let cool. Makes about 6 pints. Store for at least a month before using.

Pear

Colonel Ramsey's Apricot Chutney

Apricots have grown wild in the mountains around Beijing, China since about 2200 B.C.

The apricot was slow to spread, perhaps because it exists on the brink of viability. It must have a temperate climate, for it requires the dormant period provided by cool winters, but it blooms early and is susceptible to frost. It did progress from China to Mesopotamia, for it was grown in the hanging gardens of Babylon.

The ancient Greeks did not know of it, but the Romans did. Some scholars argue apricots were planted in Italy about the time of Nero, in the first century A.D. The Romans did not cultivate them to any great extent, as they were known to import them, which accounted for their excessive cost. They seem to have disappeared from Europe until the time of the Crusades when they were introduced to Spain, where the Moors raised them on the plains of Granada.

The apricot became familiar to the French in the 15th century, but did not arrive in England until 1562. It is stated that it reached America in the 16th century. However, it probably was introduced in quantity early in the 18th century by the Mission Fathers of California—who today produce some of our best apricots. Only 5 percent are sold fresh while 70 percent are dried. The balance is canned or made into jam.

Maj. Gray may have had a mango tree to produce the fruit for his chutney, but Col. Ramsey also has apricots for his chutney. You will enjoy this recipe for Apricot Chutney. It is best served with most meats and always with curry.

Apricot Chutney

2 1/2 pounds firm apricots (to make 7 cups, diced into 1/2-inch bits)

2 cups golden raisins

1 1/2 cups finely chopped onion

1 cup cider vinegar (or more, if needed)

1 cup water or as needed

1/2 cup dark brown sugar, packed

1 cup granulated sugar (or more, if needed)

2 teaspoons minced garlic

3 tablespoons minced fresh ginger

2 teaspoons mustard seeds

2 teaspoons ground coriander

2 cinnamon sticks, in halves

1 1/2 teaspoons ground cardamom

2 teaspoons salt

1/2 teaspoon turmeric

1/4 teaspoon cayenne

Wash apricots; dice. Discard pits. In a large copper or stainless kettle, combine apricots, raisins, onions, vinegar, water, brown

Apricot

COLONEL RAMSEY'S APRICOT CHUTNEY (CONT.)

CHAPTER

1

Relishes

sugar, granulated sugar, garlic, ginger, mustard seeds, coriander, cinnamon, cardamom, salt, turmeric and cayenne; bring to a boil. Reduce heat and continue to cook, stirring frequently, until the fruit is translucent and the chutney is thick enough to mound slightly on a spoon. You may have to add a bit more water to prevent scorching.

Taste chutney and add more sugar and vinegar, if needed. The spices will intensify as the chutney mellows in the jar. Remove cinnamon sticks. Spoon into boiling hot, clean canning jars, filling them to within 1/2 inch of the top. Seal the jars with lids and bands. Process in a boiling water bath for 10 minutes. Remove jars and cool. Let them mellow for at least 2 weeks before using— 4 weeks is better. Makes 7 half-pints.

Apricot

BEAUTIFUL BASIL

Ancient legend tells us St. Helena, mother of Emperor Constantine, was told in a vision she would find the True Cross in a place where the air was sweet with perfume. She finally discovered it under a patch of basil. The early Greeks attributed a religious character to an herb they called basilikon, meaning "kingly." At the time, custom demanded the king himself cut the first sprig of basil of the season with a golden sickle. Iron was ruled out as too common a metal.

Sweet basil is a native of India, where it was considered a sacred plant to be used in religious observances and at funerals. The Romans associated it with love and death, told in the Boccaccio story which inspired Keats' poem about Isabella, who preserved her lover's head in a pot of basil.

Basil is a pungent herb related to mint. Used in kitchens since around 400 B.C., it worked its way from Greece to France in the Middle Ages and to England in the 16th century, where it was solidly established. Its favor waned and almost disappeared from English cooking for years.

The only reminder of basil's popularity remains today in English turtle soup, which is traditionally seasoned with basil and no substitutes are allowed. It is a required ingredient in the Yugoslav national chicken soup tchorba, and always in the pesto of Italy and the pistou of Provence. Here in the United States, it is recommended as the best herb for fresh tomatoes, salads and several pasta sauces.

One of the pleasures of summer is having lots of fresh basil to make pesto. It is used on pasta, either hot or cold. Use it as a dipping sauce for crudites or on steamed vegetables and with baby new potatoes. It freezes well, but the Parmesan cheese should be omitted at the time and added after thawing and just before serving.

BASIL PESTO

4 cups fresh basil, chopped

1 cup fresh parsley, chopped

1 cup pine nuts

3/4 cup olive oil

1 stick (1/2 cup) unsalted butter, softened

2 cloves garlic, crushed

Salt and pepper

1 cup freshly grated Parmesan

In a food processor or blender, puree the basil, parsley, pine nuts, olive oil, butter, garlic, salt and pepper, and Parmesan. If you are going to freeze it, do not add Parmesan until just before serving. Pour into jars or a covered dish and refrigerate. Makes about 2 cups.

THE WONDROUS WATERMELON

Watermelons belong to the cucumber family, and have been cultivated since the time of the Pharaohs. They were a favorite food of the early prophets. The large rocks found on Mt. Carmel are called "Elijah's melons," and the story goes that the owner of the land refused to supply water to the prophet, so to punish him, Elijah turned the melons to stone.

During the Renaissance, the watermelon was the "in" fruit to enjoy. Around 1583, Ronsard praised them in his odes, and Montaigne was "excessively fond" of it. Mark Twain called the luscious fruit "chief of this world's luxuries." He wrote that when one has tasted it, he knows what the angels eat.

Watermelons can be round or oval, ranging in length from 8 to 24 inches. Their meat can be bright red, pale pink, or even yellow. Growers test the ripeness by thumping them: If the melon sounds metallic, it is not ripe.

Watermelons are eaten sliced, in chunks, in compotes, and as a garnish. A melon hollowed out and carved makes an ideal bowl for a summer compote. Watermelon pickles are popular in central Europe, where they are eaten as a dessert. They are at times spooned over ice cream.

In America, we sometimes cure (or bottle) them into a spiced pickle to use as a relish for meats.

WATERMELON PICKLES

5 pounds watermelon rind

1 tablespoon salt

8 teaspoons alum

9 cups sugar

1 quart cider vinegar

2 lemons, thinly sliced

4 cinnamon sticks (2 inches in length)

2 teaspoons whole allspice

2 teaspoons whole cloves

Cut off and discard any green and red portions from the watermelon rind, leaving only the white inner rind. Cut the rind into 1-inch pieces, enough to measure 4 quarts. Place the rind into a large enamel or stainless steel pot. Add enough water to cover; stir in salt. Bring to a boil and then reduce heat. Simmer for 15 to 20 minutes, or until the rind can be easily pierced with a fork. Remove from the heat and stir in the alum. Let cool uncovered. When cool, cover and let stand for 24 hours.

Pour off the water; rinse and drain well. Add the sugar, vinegar, lemon and cinnamon. Make a cheesecloth bag and place into it the allspice and cloves. Immerse the spice bag into the melon mixture and stir a bit. Bring to a

Watermelon

Chapter

1

Relishes

boil, stirring constantly. Remove from heat; cool, uncovered. Cover and let stand for another 24 hours. Drain the syrup into a large saucepan and bring to a boil. Pour syrup back over the rind; cover and let stand yet another 24 hours. Heat rind thoroughly in the syrup, but do not boil. Remove the spice bag and pack the rind with a cinnamon stick into sterilized jars. Heat the syrup to boiling and fill jars with the boiling syrup and seal. To ensure sealing, process 5 minutes in a boiling water bath. Makes 4 quarts.

Watermelon

Raspberry Treats

Chapter

1

Relishes

Of all the wonderful berries available, raspberries are probably the most eagerly awaited.

Their exact origin is obscure, but it is known that they were cultivated in the 16th century, although not much used in the kitchen until the 1800s—and then mainly for vinegars and syrups. The usual variety is crimson in color, but there are some types with yellow fruit as well as black and purple. All raspberries have a fruity, sharp flavor.

Raspberries should be used as soon as possible after picking or buying them, as they are highly perishable. One or two days is maximum or they will turn moldy. What's more, if stored in a deep container, the weight of the berries can crush those on the bottom. A tray, with the berries picked over and spread in a single layer, is better. Cover loosely and keep in the bottom of the refrigerator. Remove and bring to room temperature at least one hour before serving.

Traditionally raspberries are preserved by bottling or making jam. They freeze whole very successfully. Freeze only firm, ripe berries. Do not wash unless absolutely necessary. If this is necessary, hull the berries, place in a colander and dip them into cold water. Let drain and dry on a paper towel. If your berries are too ripe or juicy to freeze, they can be pureed and the puree frozen. Unsweetened puree freezes well for six months and sweetened for eight months.

Raspberry Vinegar

A wonderful raspberry vinegar may be made by adding 1 cup of berries to 2 cups white vinegar. Heat until simmering and bottle. Keep in a cool dry place for about 3 weeks and then strain the vinegar through a fine sieve. Pour back into clean bottles; add a few fresh berries and seal. A wonderful raspberry vinegar is yours for all your winter salad dressings.

Melba Sauce

The classic Melba sauce is nothing more than a slightly sweetened puree of fresh raspberries and can be made using 1 cup fresh raspberries and 3 to 4 tablespoons sifted confectioners' sugar. Crush the berries in a sieve or puree and pour into a heat-proof bowl. Set the bowl over a saucepan of hot water until the puree is just warm. Remove from heat and beat in confectioners' sugar to taste. Pour into a container; cover and chill for at least 1 hour. Serve over fresh berries or a combination of fresh berries. It is exceptionally delicious poured over ice cream or any pound cake.

Raspberry

Spring Sorrell

May is a month of glad tidings for the cook, when spring greens such as spinach and sorrell are abundant. Salmon have begun to run and fresh squid is available. Sorrell is not too easy to find in the markets, but it is easy to grow from seed. In France, it is called oseille and is most popular as an accompaniment for fish. In England, it is occasionally called sour grass. Sorrell is perishable and should be used the day it is bought or picked.

Fresh sorrell may be used to spice up a salad—a little of this lemony herb goes a long way. Most often it is consumed in soups or sauces. It loses a great deal of bulk when cooked, however; a pound of sorrell will yield less than a cup of puree. It is highly acidic and should not be cooked in an unlined aluminum or cast-iron pot.

This recipe for Sorrell Sauce is excellent for poached salmon, shad or halibut and makes about one cup sauce in a few minutes.

Sorrell Sauce

3/4 pound fresh sorrell (about 3 cups), cut
    into strips
3 tablespoons butter
1/2 cup heavy cream
Salt, black pepper, and nutmeg, as desired

Remove stems and wash sorrell. Cut the leaves into 1/2-inch ribbons. Melt the butter in large saucepan. Add sorrell and cook over medium heat, stirring 2 or 3 minutes. The sorrell will dissolve into a puree. Whisk in cream. Simmer 2 to 3 minutes. Season with salt, pepper and nutmeg to taste. Serve immediately over any good poached fish. Makes 1 cup sauce.

Milk Maid

THE SEXY MELON

All melons belong to the same species yet there are hundreds of different varieties. It seems that when it comes to cross-pollination, melons are most sexy and positively promiscuous.

Some breeds you will find in the market include:

Boule d'Or: *The name in French means golden ball and it looks like a gold-hued honeydew.*

Cantaloupe: *Named for Cantalupo, a papal garden near Tivoli, where the variety was developed. It has a fragrant orange flesh and a deeply-ridged rind. What most of us call cantaloupe is really a muskmelon.*

Casaba: *A large, round melon with a yellow, deeply-ridged rind.*

Crenshaw: *A large, round melon with a smooth, yellow rind dappled with green. These melons ripen later than most and are available into November.*

Honeydew: *This spherical fruit, with a smooth, cream colored rind is one of the most popular melons. Its sweetness is responsible for its name.*

Muskmelon: *Similar to cantaloupe, but smaller, with a netted rind and shallow ridges. Muskmelons are sweeter than cantaloupes.*

This recipe for a spicy melon relish goes beautifully with fish and chicken but does not keep well, so prepare it just for one meal.

SPICY MELON RELISH

1 ripe cantaloupe
1 ripe honeydew
1 medium cucumber
1 small red onion
4 tablespoons chopped parsley or cilantro
1 jalapeno chile, or to taste
Juice of 1 or 2 limes

Cut the melons into quarters and remove seeds. Cut away the rind and dice the flesh into 1/4-inch cubes. You will only need 1 cup of each melon. The excess may be used in a salad. Peel, seed and dice the cucumber. Finely chop the onion and parsley or cilantro. Seed and mince as much chile as your taste suggests.

Two hours before serving, combine ingredients, adding the lime juice and chile to taste. The relish will be sweet from the melon and a bit sour and spicy. Store in a cool place or the refrigerator before serving. Serves 6. This recipe makes about 3 cups.

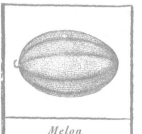

Melon

More Than You Wanted To Know About Horseradish

Horseradish is a hardy perennial plant of the mustard family. It owes its pungency to the volatile mustard oils that form when it is exposed to air. The origin of this root is not really known. The Egyptians knew of it, for it was listed as part of the diet of the pyramid builders. It was in use in Egypt at the time of the Exodus about 1500 B.C., as we are told that it was one of the five bitter herbs which the Jews ate at Passover. (The other four included coriander, lettuce, horehound and nettles.) There was no clear distinction between the radish and the horseradish until Palladium pointed out the differences in the fourth century A.D.

Horseradish's true place of origin is difficult to determine, as it became transported all over the world. It has been attributed to the Mediterranean area, southeastern Europe, and western Asia and the Orient. Today, one would guess that it originated not far from the area where it is the most consumed and most appreciated: Germany. It spread northward to Scandinavia and westward to England during the Renaissance. It was first mentioned in America as a food in the 16th century, but was known as a medicine as early as the 13th century.

An English writer of the time noted that, in Germany, horseradish was used to make a sauce to eat with fish and meats as the English used mustard. In 1640, it was referred to in England as a staple of country folk and strong laboring men because it was too strong for more tender and gentle stomachs. Shortly after, it became a standard accompaniment for beef even on the tables of those with "tender and gentle stomachs."

It was brought to America by the early settlers, but was not listed as a common edible plant until 1806. The hot, biting taste and pungent aroma do not exist in the unbroken root but rather are developed during the grating by a chemical reaction found in the cells of the growing plant. Horseradish has to be grated fine before it has much flavor.

Horseradish spices up salads, sauces, juices, soups and mayonnaise. It is great with raw oysters, broiled fish, roast meats and smoked foods. Preparing horseradish only requires a few minutes, so do not make up too much at a time or it will lose its character.

Chapter

1

Relishes

Fresh Horseradish

Several inches of fresh horseradish root, peeled

1/4 cup vinegar (distilled white or white wine)

Salt and sugar, as needed

Peel the root and remove any green tinges. Cut into 1/2-inch pieces. Add a handful at a time to the processor with the vinegar. Process until just grated, not to a pulp. Pour this first batch into a strainer over a bowl. Return the vinegar to the processor bowl and add more horseradish. Continue to process in batches, straining and reusing the vinegar.

Combine vinegar with the grating; stir in more vinegar if needed. Season with salt and sugar, about a pinch of each to each 1/2 inch of horseradish and juice. The sugar is meant to add smoothness to the flavor, not added as a sweetener. Store in glass jars, closely covered, in refrigerator. Will keep several weeks.

Sauce

3 1/2 tablespoons prepared horseradish, rinsed, drained and squeezed dry

3 tablespoons mayonnaise

1 tablespoon tarragon vinegar

1 teaspoon Dijon mustard

1 1/4 teaspoons sugar

1/2 teaspoon salt

Dash of pepper

1/4 of a Granny Smith apple, grated

In a bowl, combine horseradish, mayonnaise, vinegar, mustard, sugar, salt, and pepper; whisk to blend. Fold in grated apple. Refrigerate covered for a few hours. Makes 1 cup.

Hot Horseradish Sauce

2 horseradish roots (enough to make 2 cups)

1/2 cup white wine vinegar

4 tablespoons dry white wine

Peel the roots and grate with a fine grater or finely chop in a food processor. Mix in vinegar and wine. Store in glass jars in refrigerator. It will keep for at least 3 months.

If you need a cocktail sauce, mix equal parts of the sauce with ketchup; for a sauce with meats, mix with whipped cream and 2 tablespoons mayonnaise; for a spread, mix with cream cheese and grated cheddar cheese.

THE ASPARAGUS STORY

Early generations called them the "scepters of Venus." Moncelot wrote that when asparagus appears, "surely spring has sent its calling card on a plate." And Julia Child has referred to asparagus as the beautiful "luxury vegetable" that can stand on its own as a separate course in any meal.

There are at least 14 species of asparagus. The green variety is the best known in America. In France, they go to great lengths to grow white asparagus, burying the stalks with fresh earth as they grow to keep their anemic complexion. However, I find it tends to be bland and fibrous.

When buying asparagus, try to find unblemished, bright-green stalks with closed, compact tips and stalks that are uniform in size. If you do not plan to use it the same day you buy it, store it upright in a container in about 2 inches of water. The butt end should be cut off to let a fresh cut be in the water. Cover the container with a plastic bag to retain the moisture. It should keep fresh for a day or two.

Julia feels it is cruel to bend the stems until they break. The stalk should be peeled toward the butt end for the whole stalk. This way the long peeled stalks are elegant to serve. Peeled asparagus also cooks quicker and remains green and fresh. It is not necessary to have a round cooker so that the tips steam and the butts boil. A large skillet with enough salted, boiling water to cover them is just right. Remove the spears from the water and arrange on a napkin or cloth-covered platter and let them drain. If serving them hot, they should be placed on a warm platter while making the sauce. If served cold, drain on a towel and then transfer to a cold platter and season with a vinaigrette dressing to help keep them green. A garnish of finely chopped hard-cooked egg sprinkled on the tip end is good.

Hot asparagus may be served with just melted butter or a hot sauce such as hollandaise, or with a lemon butter sauce or Maltaise sauce, which is a bit different and is made with orange juice in place of the lemon juice in a hollandaise.

ORANGE MALTAISE SAUCE

3/4 cup butter

4 egg yolks

Juice of 1 orange, or to taste

Salt, white pepper, cayenne

Melt the butter in a small saucepan over low heat. Set aside in a warm place. Place the egg yolks and 1 tablespoon orange juice in a large stainless steel bowl. Whisk together vigorously for about a minute over a simmering pan of water. The mixture will

Asparagus

The Asparagus Story (cont.)

Chapter

1

Relishes

become light and as you continue to whisk should thicken to the consistency of mayonnaise. As soon as the sauce begins to thicken, remove it from the heat. If the mixture starts to get too thick, place it over a pan of cold water.

Add the warm butter in a thin stream, whisking constantly. It is better to add the butter slowly than too quickly. Add the rest of the orange juice, a few drops at a time, and continue to whisk. Season with salt, white pepper and a bit of cayenne. If it is too sweet, add a few drops of lemon juice. If it requires a stronger orange flavor, add more orange juice. Serve over the hot asparagus or pass separately. The sauce is highly seasoned.

Asparagus

The Delight of Cranberries

Chapter

1

Relishes

The cranberry season starts in late September and continues through November. The later the harvest, the darker the berry. They are a uniquely American food.

Cranberry sauce was invented by the American Indians. The cranberry was an important food for them before the first European arrived, and they ate them raw as well as cooked. When the Indians cooked them, they sweetened them with maple syrup or honey.

When sugarcane plantations were established in the West Indies, the Europeans contributed to the dish and appreciated it as much as the Indians. When John Jossely visited New England in 1639, he reported on cranberries more accurately than when he told of seeing a mermaid in Maine's Casco Bay: "The Indians and English use them much, boyling them with sugar for Sauce to eat with their Meat, and it is a delicious Sauce."

Cranberries will keep well inasmuch as they are protected by their high acidity—and, it is for this reason they were perhaps the first American fruit to be shipped to Europe commercially. Early in the 18th century, "Cape Cod bell cranberries" were being sold on the Strand in London, at what must have been a fancy price in those days, four shillings a jar. From England, the cranberry spread to France, where it gained little favor, but was popular and appreciated throughout Germany. Cranberries will keep for up to 10 days in the refrigerator and can be frozen almost indefinitely. They are good for you because of their high vitamin C content.

It takes about 10 minutes to make fresh cranberry sauce. Once you know how easy it is to concoct, you will be embarrassed to use the canned stuff. This spicy cranberry sauce will keep for up to three weeks in the refrigerator.

Gingered Cranberry Sauce

1 pound fresh cranberries, washed and
    picked clean
1/2 cup sugar or to taste
3 strips lemon peel
2 sticks cinnamon
1/2-inch piece fresh ginger, peeled, and
    sliced thin
1/4 cup apple cider

1/4 cup ginger brandy (or orange juice or
    cider)

Combine the cranberries, sugar, lemon peel, cinnamon, ginger, apple cider and ginger brandy in a large saucepan. Bring to a boil; reduce heat and let cool. Refrigerate when cooled. For extra flavor, leave lemon peel, cinnamon and ginger in sauce until serving time.

Cranberries

DELICIOUS FOOD GIFTS

CHAPTER 1

Relishes

One of the real compliments of our time is to be invited to someone's home for dinner or a special weekend visit. A gracious way to show appreciation is to take along a small gift, and a food gift makes a perfect choice, especially during the holidays.

Be sure to keep in mind that the gift should be something that can easily be served at any time. Try to select an item that the host or hostess will not feel obligated to fit into the planned menu. A surprise gift that must be served right away may be more of a complication than a compliment.

Give a food gift that keeps well, travels well and is attractive and tasty. Dress it up with a doily, a ribbon, a pretty piece of fabric, or package the gift in a container that will make a second gift.

The following two recipes make ideal gifts.

CRANBERRY CONSERVE

4 cups fresh cranberries (washed and picked over)
1 cup water
1 orange
3 1/2 cups sugar
2 cups peeled, diced apple
1/2 cup raisins
2/3 cup chopped pecans

Combine the cranberries and water in a large saucepan; bring to a boil. Cover, reduce heat, and simmer for about 7 minutes or until the skins pop.

Grate orange peel; seed and dice orange. Add the orange peel and diced orange, sugar, apple, raisins and pecans to cranberries; mix well. Cook until mixture thickens, about 30 minutes over medium heat, stirring often. Remove from heat; cool. Spoon into jars or a selected container. Store in refrigerator. Makes about 6 cups.

MUSTARD SAUCE

1 stick (1/2 cup) butter
2 tablespoons flour
1/2 cup prepared mustard
1/2 cup vinegar
1 1/2 cups sugar
1 can (10 3/4 ounces) beef bouillon

Melt the butter; stir in flour until well mixed. Add mustard, vinegar, sugar and beef bouillon, blending thoroughly. Stir and cook for 10 minutes, stirring occasionally. Remove from heat; cool.

Pour this sauce into decorative glasses or jars. Cover and refrigerate until needed. Decorate container for the occasion or season. Store in refrigerator. Will keep for several weeks.

Conserve

CHAPTER 2

The Splendid Salad

Lettuce

Pepper Pot

Peas

Orange Tree

CRANBERRY RING MOLD

CHAPTER 2

The Splendid Salad

Christmas dining in the White House has not varied much through the years. The sumptuous repasts have always been an integral part of the season. Washington and Madison customarily served eggnog; Jefferson served hot spiced brandy toddy; Teddy Roosevelt loved champagne with his chicken sandwiches; and Franklin Delano Roosevelt shared his uncle's partiality to champagne.

The Carter family spent their Christmas with families in Plains, Ga. Early in the morning Christmas day, the entire clan retired to Miss Lillian's house, where the president's mother laid on a Southern holiday breakfast of country ham, eggs, grits with cheese, homemade strawberry preserves, hot biscuits and coffee.

Later in the day, the family moved on to the home of Miss Allie, Rosalynn Carter's mother. There a gargantuan feast took place. The menu consisted of a relish tray of celery hearts, carrot sticks, homemade pickles, homemade pickled peaches and watermelon rind preserves, followed by roast turkey with cornbread stuffing, rice, giblet gravy, candied sweet potatoes, green beans, cheese ring filled with strawberry preserves, a cranberry ring mold filled with apple-pecan salad, hot rolls, fruit cake, ambrosia and coffee. Miss Allie's recipe for cranberry mold was the all-time family favorite.

MISS ALLIE'S CRANBERRY RING MOLD

2 envelopes unflavored gelatin

1/2 cup cold water

3/4 cup boiling water

1/4 cup fresh lemon juice

2 cans jellied cranberry sauce

1/2 cup cold water

1/2 teaspoon horseradish

Dash of Tabasco

1/4 teaspoon salt

In a large bowl, sprinkle the gelatin over the 1/2 cup cold water to soften. Add boiling water and stir to dissolve the gelatin. Stir in lemon juice.

In a saucepan, combine the cranberry sauce with 1/2 cup cold water. Stir and then whisk until smooth; do not allow to boil. Add the horseradish, Tabasco and salt. Stir in the gelatin mixture until dissolved. Pour into a 6-cup ring mold that has been rinsed with cold water. Chill for 4 hours.

Cranberries

The Fruitful Orange

Chapter 2

The Splendid Salad

Citrus fruit in the winter was once relatively rare. In our parents' time, a treat of an orange received in the Christmas stocking was something special. This custom also reminds us that winter is the best time to eat them.

The orange tree is one of the few that simultaneously bears leaves, flowers and fruit. Today, the orange blossom is still considered a symbol of innocence and fertility and is always popular with brides to ensure a fruitful marriage.

The Chinese domesticated the orange in commercial groves as early as 2400 B.C. The fruit was a status symbol in Europe through the 18th century. Every self-respecting chateau or palace had its own orangerie, citrus greenhouse. The orangerie at Versailles had 1,200 silver tubs planted with oranges. The fruit was more for show than for eating, but was eaten on special occasions.

Oranges become sweeter the longer they stay on the tree. Orange trees are most vulnerable to cold and will freeze at 28 degrees in about four hours. In America, many people believe the best oranges and grapefruit come from Florida. In their favor I will say the area known as the Indian River region of central Florida does have a special soil condition and a particularly mild climate that enables the fruit to stay on the tree in order to ripen to its peak.

In Sicily, oranges are available most of the year, and if they are a bit short they have Tunisia, just across the sea, which produces fine oranges and can ship overnight. A popular dish served at lunchtime or as an accompaniment for fish is this Orange-Pine Nut Salad.

Orange-Pine Nut Salad

8 plump, juicy oranges
1 clove garlic
4 tablespoons olive oil
6 to 8 tablespoons red wine vinegar
4 tablespoons toasted pine nuts
1/4 teaspoon dried red pepper
Salt and pepper to taste

Peel and skin oranges. Cut segments away from the membranes, while working over a bowl to save juice. Cut garlic in half and use one half to rub the inside of glass or ceramic mixing bowl. Place oranges and juice with garlic in the bowl with the oil, vinegar, pine nuts, red pepper (taste after a bit is added, then add as desired), salt and pepper. Extra vinegar and oil may be added, if needed. Taste, then marinate for 10 minutes. Remove garlic before serving on a bed of lettuce.

Orange Tree

A Bright Salad

During October the pomegranate returns to our markets from the warmer climates. In many cultures, this multi-seeded, scarlet fruit is the symbol of fertility. In Turkey, young women drop the fruit on the ground; the number of seeds that break out of the fruit is supposed to foretell the number of children she will have.

When selecting a pomegranate, look for a large round fruit with unblemished skin. It should feel heavy. Avoid any with soft spots or split skins.

The Waldorf salad remains a favorite autumn salad after many years. It was created by Oscar Tschirky to honor the opening of the famous hotel in 1893. This version has a different twist in that pomegranate seeds replace the celery, and the juice is used to freshen up the dressing.

Chapter 2

The Splendid Salad

Pomegranate Waldorf Salad

2 pomegranates

1 large crisp apple

1 ripe pear

Juice of 1/2 lemon

1/2 cup pecans, broken

2 tablespoons chopped fresh chives

Dressing

Break one of the pomegranates and remove the seeds. Cut the other one in half and extract the juice, using a reamer. Peel and core the apple and pear. Dice into 1/2-inch pieces. Sprinkle fruit with lemon juice. Lightly toast the pecans in preheated 400 degree oven; toss with fruit mixture.

Dressing

Juice from 1 pomegranate

3 tablespoons mayonnaise

2 teaspoons balsamic vinegar

1 tablespoon walnut oil

Salt and black pepper

Honey, if needed

In a large bowl, mix the pomegranate juice, mayonnaise, balsamic vinegar, walnut oil, salt, pepper and honey (if dressing is too tart). Add fruit and nuts; toss lightly. Serve on a bed of lettuce.

Dressing

PALACE HOTEL SALAD

CHAPTER 2

The Splendid Salad

One of the great salads of all time was invented at the legendary Palace Hotel in San Francisco, which was destroyed in the earthquake and fire of 1906. The dressing is the reason for the salad.

PALACE HOTEL SALAD

1 head butter lettuce
1 bunch watercress

DRESSING

1/2 cup good thick mayonnaise
2 anchovy fillets, mashed
2 tablespoons parsley, minced
2 tablespoons green onion tops, chopped
1 clove garlic, crushed
1 tablespoon lemon juice
1 tablespoon tarragon vinegar
3 tablespoons whipped cream
Salt and black pepper

Carefully wash and dry lettuce leaves. Wash the watercress gently, removing any damaged or yellow leaves. Trim the stems and shake to dry. Gently roll the lettuce and watercress in a slightly damp cloth and chill for at least 1 hour.

To make the dressing, place the first 7 ingredients in a bowl and beat with a wooden spoon until well mixed. Fold in the cream and season with salt and freshly ground black pepper. Cover the bowl and chill until you are ready to assemble the salad.

Tear the lettuce into large pieces, and place in a salad bowl. Divide the watercress into sprigs and set aside. Spoon about one-third of the dressing over the lettuce and toss until the leaves are lightly coated. Arrange the watercress around the edge of the bowl and serve immediately with the rest of the dressing in a separate bowl so people can help themselves to more. Serves 6.

And do let your mind be boggled by the additions one may make to this or any salad to achieve more color, variety and flavor. The list could include celery, green pepper, onions or shallots or you can try tomatoes (peeled, of course), cucumbers (also peeled), radishes, mushrooms, avocado, nuts, raisins, crumbled bacon or slices of hard-boiled egg.

Lettuce

THE VERSATILE PEPPER

CHAPTER 2

The Splendid Salad

The real winner of the "American nouvelle cuisine" has to be the bell pepper. The sudden rise in the pepper's prestige was heightened by our interest in ethnic cuisine. Peppers figure prominently in the cooking of Spain, Italy, Eastern Europe and the American Southwest. America' s fine young chefs learned the age-old technique of roasting peppers to remove the skins, to bring out the pepper's natural sweetness.

Peppers are good for you; a medium red pepper contains a good supply of vitamin A and vitamin C. Bell peppers come in a rainbow of hues; green, red, brown, black, purple and yellow. Today, they turn up in the finest restaurants, roasted, grilled, marinated, pureed and served in any number of ways.

The pepper is native to the Americas. European explorers introduced the milder varieties to Europe and the fiery ones to Asia. The term "pepper" is a misnomer, coined by Columbus after he tasted one of the hot varieties, since one of his goals was to discover a quicker route to the source of spices, India.

This salad is a simple, but visual delight. It uses red and yellow bell peppers and the slenderest green beans you can find—haricot verts, if possible.

Pepper Salad with Green Beans

1 large yellow bell pepper
1 large red bell pepper
1 pound slender green beans
1 teaspoon Dijon mustard
1 tablespoon balsamic vinegar
1/8 teaspoon salt
Fresh black pepper to taste
1 tablespoon chopped fresh herbs (dill, tarragon, basil)
4 tablespoons olive oil

Core and seed the peppers; cut lengthwise into 1/4-inch strips. Snap off ends of the beans. Blanch the pepper strips in boiling salted water for 15 seconds, then transfer with a slotted spoon to a colander and refresh under cold water. Cook the beans in the same boiling water for a few minutes or until crisp-tender. Drain and refresh under cold water

Prepare herb vinaigrette by placing in the bottom of a salad bowl the mustard, vinegar, salt, pepper and herbs; whisk into a smooth paste. Gradually whisk in the oil until thickened. Add the beans and peppers and toss to mix. Chill before serving. Serves 4.

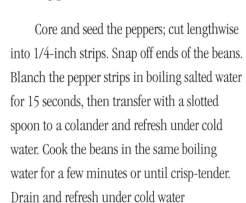

EVEN IN THE OLD TESTAMENT

CHAPTER 2

The Splendid Salad

Almonds have to be the most popular nuts used in cooking. Be they whole, sliced or ground, they lend their flavor equally well to spicy dishes, vegetables, salads or sweet desserts.

Almonds are mentioned throughout the Old Testament. They were known to the Romans as "the Greek nut." During the 18th century, they were popular as a sweet. Cakes made from them were known as marchpanes, which today has been corrupted into the word marzipan. When whole almonds are sugar-coated, they are called dragees.

Almonds grow best in hot, dry climates. The countries that produce the most almonds are Sicily, Spain, South Africa and Australia. California produces almonds in this country.

There are two types of almonds—bitter and sweet. The bitter variety is used to make essences, flavorings and oils. It should not be eaten. The sweet one is the edible nut and is used in all forms of recipes.

A quick main course that is substantial and colorful is this salad served with a baked potato and/or bran muffins.

ALMOND, AVOCADO AND CHEESE SALAD

1/2 cup blanched almonds, sliced or chopped

2 ripe avocados

9 ounces Cheddar cheese

2 medium tomatoes

1/2 cucumber, peeled, and seeded

6 green onions, chopped

1 tablespoon thyme

1 tablespoon chopped parsley

4 tablespoons olive oil

2 tablespoons white wine vinegar

1 tablespoon tomato puree

1 garlic clove, minced

2 drops Tabasco

Lettuce leaves

Blanch almonds; slice or chop. Peel and stone avocados; dice. Chop cheese and tomatoes into pieces about the size of the diced avocado and put into a bowl with almonds, cucumber, onions, thyme and parsley. In small bowl, beat oil, vinegar, tomato puree, garlic and Tabasco until emulsified. Taste and season with salt and pepper; fold dressing into avocado mixture. Line a salad bowl with lettuce leaves; pile salad inside. Makes 4 servings.

Almonds

ALL ABOUT PASTA

Dried pasta comes in an exciting assortment of sizes and shapes. In addition to the well-known spaghetti, there are tubes, shells, wheels, stars and butterflies.

The Chinese have made pasta since at least 1100 B.C. As a point of pride, the Italians insist that they invented pasta in their part of the world. The first clear reference to a noodle of any kind is in the fifth century from Jerusalem and written in Aramaic. This has been questioned, since the use of noodles could have violated Jewish dietary laws.

The use of macaroni and lasagna in Italy is documented before 1295 when Marco Polo returned from China. When he was introduced to noodles in China he spoke of lasagna, which indicates that he was already familiar with the food.

The pasta industry developed in the 18th century around Naples, which had a perfect climate for drying pasta. The mild sea breezes and the hot winds from Mount Vesuvius ensured that the pasta would not dry too slowly and become moldy, or too fast and crack and break. The number of shops making pasta in Naples quickly went from 60 to 280 between the years 1700 and 1785.

With more than 600 different pasta shapes and a variety of names, it would be easy to give several shapes of pasta, packaged and bowed, as a Christmas gift along with a pasta recipe.

The bright colors of the salami, pepper and tomatoes contrast well with the pale pasta shells used in this salad.

CHAPTER 2

The Splendid Salad

PASTA SALAD

8 ounces pasta shells, medium size (called conchiglie), cooked and drained

1 green pepper, seeded

4 spring onions, chopped

4 medium tomatoes, seeded, skinned and coarsely chopped

4 ounces sliced Italian salami

1/2 cup cooked corn

4 tablespoons mayonnaise

2 tablespoons cream

Salt and pepper to taste

Cook pasta; drain. Shred green pepper; chop onions and tomatoes coarsely. Cut salami into strips.

Add to pasta the green pepper, onions, tomatoes, salami and corn. Thin mayonnaise with cream; add salt and pepper to taste. Mix mayonnaise mixture thoroughly with pasta mixture; taste for seasoning. Chill and serve. Makes 4 to 6 servings.

Tomato

MACARONI AND MORE

CHAPTER 2

The Splendid Salad

Maccheroni, as the Italians spelled it, was a generic term for any flour-and-water pasta, whether rolled flat like lasagna, shaped into long hollow tubes like cannelloni, or squeezed into thin strands like spaghetti. In Rome, they were rolling out these floury pastas long before Marco Polo discovered the Chinese were rolling egg rolls, noodles and won tons.

Unstuffed pasta did not become a major dish until the time of the great Italian chef Corrado, which coincided with the invention of the first pasta machine in the 18th century. By the latter part of that century, Naples and Genoa began mass production of maccheroni.

Thomas Jefferson always was aware of continental foods, so in 1789 he sent his protege William Short to Naples to bring back a "macaroni mould" for his kitchen. Upon his arrival in Italy, Short wrote to Jefferson that he had found a mold, but it produced a pasta that was smaller than those used to manufacture macaroni. He had found a spaghetti mold with thin tubes that were more fashionable than the larger ones. The new macaroni required a newfangled table instrument, the three-pronged fork, to eat spaghetti in a more refined manner than could be managed with the hands. Short returned to America with the new mold—and a supply of forks.

In Jefferson's receipt book at Monticello, he explains that the noodles could be used to thicken a soup, or if you wanted to dress them as macaroni, they should be dropped in boiling water for 15 minutes and then drained and tossed with a new dressing of butter and cheese and served as a separate course.

Today, macaroni and spaghetti are no longer the generic term for Italian pasta. When Yankee Doodle went to London and "stuck a feather in his hat and called it macaroni," he never dreamed at some later day we would have to distinguish macaroni from rigatoni, fettuccine, penne, ravioli, linguine, tagliatelle and tortellini.

This recipe for a macaroni salad would be in good standing in any fashionable pasta club.

Yankee Doodle

Macaroni and More (cont.)

Macaroni Calico Salad

2 cups cooked macaroni

1/4 cup olive oil

1 tablespoon lemon juice

1 small zucchini, diced

1 medium tomato, peeled and diced

3 green onions, chopped

1 each roasted and diced, red and green
  pepper

1 cup cubed Cheddar cheese

1 cup minced parsley

1 cup plain yogurt

1 teaspoon salt

1/2 teaspoon pepper

Pinch of cayenne

1/4 cup diced chives

1/2 cup sliced, stuffed olives

In a large bowl, toss the macaroni with oil
and lemon juice. Add zucchini, tomato,
onions, peppers, cheese, parsley, yogurt, salt,
pepper, cayenne, chives and olives; toss
thoroughly. Cover and chill at least 2 hours
before serving. Makes 6 to 8 servings.

Chapter 2

The Splendid Salad

Yankee Doodle

A Buchanan Family Favorite

Chapter 2

The Splendid Salad

With the election of James Buchanan, gaiety returned to the White House. The ban on social activities, such as dancing, eating and drinking at receptions, was lifted.

Although he was a bachelor, he was not an abandoned man, for he had his niece Harriet Lane as his great asset. She was a lovely blonde with violet eyes, a tall, slim figure, and the grace and social attributes of a princess. In short order, she became the toast of Washington society. When Buchanan was ambassador to the Court of St. James, Harriet accompanied him and was able to cope with London society so well she became much adored by Queen Victoria.

Shortly after Buchanan settled into the White House, he learned that the Prince of Wales was going to visit Canada and wrote to Queen Victoria inviting the prince to visit the United States. The stay of Albert Edward, Prince of Wales, who later was to become King Edward VII, brought about the biggest social event at the White House. For decades afterward, social commentators were rehashing it breathlessly.

Buchanan's salary was not enough to compensate for his elaborate entertaining, and to quiet his critics or those who were not invited, he was forced to pay the bills for his lavish dinners and receptions out of his own pocket.

At one of the parties, 500 quarts of chicken salad were served. The Buchanan version of chicken salad, however, was quite different from many of today's recipes. It illustrates the evolution of chicken salad through American history.

Buchanan-Lane Chicken Salad

2 medium-size chickens

1 teaspoon salt

1 stalk celery

8 eggs

1 cup oil (olive or peanut)

1/2 cup vinegar

1 tablespoon dry mustard

Salt and pepper to taste

In a large pot, boil the chickens in water with 1 teaspoon salt. When tender, allow to cool, then cut meat into 1/4-inch squares. Set aside. Chop celery into small pieces and chill in cold water. Cook eggs until hard; cool. Remove yolks ("yelks" in the original recipe) and mash them with the oil. Add vinegar, mustard, salt and pepper. Mix well. Dry celery and set aside. In a large bowl, mix celery, chicken, and chopped egg whites. Add egg-yolk mixture and mix well, but lightly. Chill until ready to serve. Serves 12.

Hen

A New Year Tradition

The tradition of eating black-eyed peas on new Year's Day may have had its roots in the Civil War. There are hundreds of tales that explain why you should eat black-eyed peas, but the one thing that ties them together is that they are all supposed to bring luck and money during the new year.

When General William Sherman's troops blazed their way across the South during the Civil War, the smokehouses and granaries were the primary targets for the Northern invaders. Most of the meat was taken. The hog jowl, the least meaty piece of the hog, was most often left behind. At this time a Southern family was considered lucky to have some black-eyed peas and a hog jowl to serve.

Andrew Jackson and Andrew Johnson were both born in North Carolina and felt strongly about the tradition. Both Andrews served black-eyed peas at the White House on New Year's Day. They added rice to the dish and called it Hopping John. President Eisenhower and wife Mamie, had it served during their reign at the White House.

Modern day cooks continue the tradition to assure luck, health and money. The Department of Agriculture lists it as a great source of carbohydrates for energy besides containing B vitamins and significant amounts of iron, calcium and protein.

In order to assure you of good health, luck and money, try this recipe using the peas for the coins and the greens for the folding money.

Black-Eyed Peas Salad

1 1/2 cups cooked rice

2 cups cooked black-eyed peas

1 cup celery, chopped

1/2 cup coconut, toasted

1 cup pickled peaches, sliced

1 cup red, seedless grapes

1 1/2 cups mayonnaise

1/2 cup chopped chutney

1 teaspoon chili powder

3-4 teaspoons lime juice

1 banana, sliced

Lettuce leaves

Cook the rice and set aside. Cook the peas and when done and most of the liquid is absorbed add the rice, celery, and chili powder. Cook over very low heat till hot. Remove from heat and chill.

In a large bowl, mix the rice and peas mixture with the coconut. In a small bowl mix the mayonnaise, chutney, and lime juice. Mix with the rice mixture and gently toss in the peaches, grapes and banana. Serve on a bed of lettuce.

Grapes

A New Variety

Chapter 2

The Splendid Salad

The hot days of summer call for an easy, make-ahead and cool meal. When the temperature hits the 90s, it's the time to think about a cold supper. I tried one of those store-bought barbecued turkey breasts to accompany this spice apple and potato salad.

Spice Apple and Potato Salad

2 pounds new potatoes

Salt to taste

1 bay leaf

8 slices bacon, diced

1 Spanish onion, chopped

1 1/2 tablespoons sugar

4 tablespoons vinegar

2 teaspoons Worcestershire sauce

1/2 cup olive oil

Dash of Tabasco

Black pepper and salt to taste

1 pound tart apples

Lemon juice

Boil the potatoes in their skins in salted water with 1 bay leaf until just cooked. Drain and cool until they can be peeled. Dice and set aside.

Fry the bacon in a skillet until bacon bits are crisp. Remove and drain on a paper towel. Combine the bacon, onion, sugar, vinegar, and Worcestershire in a pan and heat until hot, but not boiling. Stir in the olive oil, Tabasco, salt and pepper to taste.

Toss the potatoes with this sauce and let them cool and chill. Quarter and core the apples and slice into a bowl of water with a bit of lemon juice to prevent discoloration.

Just before serving, drain any excess sauce from the potatoes. Dry the apples, and toss with the potatoes. Season with salt and pepper. Serve with cold roast turkey, beef or ham. Serves 8.

Pepper Pot

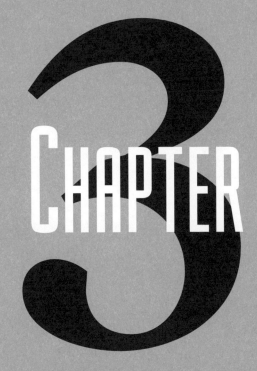

CHAPTER 3

Super Soups

Clam

Turkey

Corn

Cherries

The Scoop on Soup

Soups are for all occasions. When served with chunks of bread and cheese, a hot, hearty soup makes a perfect midday snack or supper for all the family.

Soups are capable of great variety, and most involve very little effort. You can begin them almost without thinking because if you make an error along the way, it is easily corrected. Too thick? Add water, milk or cream. Too thin? Any thickener will take care of that. No time to chop vegetables? A few seconds in a processor can change an unappealing mass of cooked vegetables into a tantalizing cream soup.

When putting together a soup, the most important rule is to please yourself. A soup is a welcome chance to use the leftovers in the refrigerator as a start, but ingredients from cans, packets, bottles and surprises from the freezer are equally suitable. Traditionally, the liquid used for cooking vegetables becomes the basis for tasty, nutritious soups. Any stock from meat or poultry may be used. The water from beans is particularly good as is cauliflower water, which has a strong flavor but combines well.

A few tips that may be overlooked when making a soup: Shriveled vegetables that are not in their prime are good candidates for the soup pot. Just chop them and add to a well-flavored stock. Or chop and saute in oil, then simmer in a bit of water until tender. Blend or puree them and add to the soup as needed. To thicken a watery soup, make a paste of butter and flour and whisk into the soup. Or whisk in a cubed boiled potato. To add body, you may throw in some morsels of rice or pasta bits. To add flavor, blend in a stock cube or add some sherry, wine or dry Marsala, or even a bit of wine vinegar if you are discreet.

Common garnishes are toasted croutons, crisp bacon bits, chopped parsley, a slice of lemon or cucumber or watercress leaves.

This good curry soup can be made in about 35 minutes. It is ideal for a cold day.

Curried Mushroom Soup

6 tablespoons butter, divided
1 small onion, chopped
1 1/2 cups chopped mushrooms
3 1/2 cups chicken stock
2 tablespoons flour

1/2 teaspoon curry powder
Salt to taste
Black pepper
1/2 cup thin cream (half and half)
2 tablespoons sherry
Chopped fresh parsley

Mushrooms

Curried Mushroom Soup (cont.)

Chapter 3

Super Soups

In a soup kettle, melt 4 tablespoons of the butter; saute the onion and mushrooms about 3 minutes. Pour in chicken stock; simmer, covered for 15 minutes. Meanwhile, melt the remaining butter in a small saucepan; add flour. Cook for a minute. Add 1/2 cup of the hot mushroom mixture. Stir in curry. Season with salt and pepper. Return to heat and heat until rich and smooth. Pour contents of the small pan into the large kettle with mushroom mixture and mix well. Stir in cream and sherry and heat through. Do not boil. Serve in warmed soup bowls. Garnish with chopped parsley. Serves 6.

Mushrooms

Terrific Turkey Soup

Benjamin Franklin wished the turkey had been chosen as the representative of our country. He wrote to his daughter that he thought "the eagle was a bird of bad moral character; like those among men who live by sharping and robbing, he is generally poor, and often very lousy. The turkey is a much more respectable bird, and withal a true original native of America."

Franklin even advocated putting the turkey on the American flag. Being referred to as a true American native, however, should be taken in a broader sense by referring to the New World. The turkey was probably not a native of any territory now included within the United States, but of Mexico.

References are made to a large bird served by the Greeks and Romans. Most scholars of the time contested this and have said it was probably guinea hen.

A tapestry dating to 1087 pictures a turkey in the marginal decorations. The Bayeaux Tapestry made during this time was Norman. It is known that the Norsemen maintained settlements in North America, within the turkey's range, from the years 985 to 1123. It could be that these men brought back sketches of this strange and unknown fowl, but not specimens of the bird itself. Brillat-Savarin points out that the turkey was known in France as the "hen of India," meaning the West Indies. Most 16th century chronicles agree with him.

During the conquest of Mexico, Cortez reported that when he visited the Tlateloloco market "they were selling fowls and birds with great dewlaps." Las Casas wrote that during the Cordoba expedition, the Indians brought them large roasted hens, as big as peacocks but better eating, whose distinctive feature was a large dewlap. (Could this have been the real beginning of fast-food service?)

Columbus did not bring the turkey back from his voyage, as there were none on the Caribbean Islands. The earliest mention of them in Spain was in 1511 by Miguel de Passamonte who was instructed by the Bishop of Valencia to bring turkeys to Spain. He returned with 10 birds. In 1513, when Ponce de Leon landed in Florida, they were plentiful, but he did not collect them for he was not looking for food. Both Cordoba and Cortez saw them in Mexico in 1517 and 1519; neither sent them home. Coronado mentions having seen them in 1540 and 1541 in the Indian pueblos, but he was too busy searching for the Seven Cities of Cibola to send one home, and by this time the turkey was already gracing the tables of Europe.

Everyone has his own way of cooking a whole turkey. To me, the leftovers are the

Turkey

TERRIFIC TURKEY SOUP (CONT.)

CHAPTER 3

Super Soups

best part. If you did not cook your own turkey, I hope you can beg for some of the leftover carcass from friend or host. The trick to this turkey stock soup is to cook it at the gentlest simmer, conscientiously skimming off any fat. If the stock is allowed to boil, the fat will homogenize with the broth, making it cloudy and oily.

Turkey Noodle Soup

Stock

Carcass from a 10- to 12-pound turkey
1 large onion
1 parsnip (optional)
2 carrots
2 celery sticks
2 cloves garlic
Bouquet garni (bay leaf, thyme, parsley,
    peppercorn, 1 clove)
1 tablespoon tomato paste (optional)
noodles

Remove the skin and fat from the carcass and place bones in a large stockpot. Cut the onion in quarters, leaving the skin on. Cut the parsnip, carrots and celery into chunks. Peel the garlic. Add all vegetables to the pot. Add the bouquet garni and tomato paste to the pot with enough water to cover the bones.

Place over high heat and bring to a boil. Skim off the foam and reduce heat. Gently simmer for 2 to 3 hours. Strain into a large bowl, pressing the bones and vegetables to extract flavors. Let the stock cool at room temperature. Skim off any fat. Will keep for 4 or 5 days in the refrigerator.

To make the broth and soup, season stock with salt and pepper. Cook 1 pound of good noodles in a separate pot until *al dente*. Heat the broth and add hot cooked noodles. Ladle into a bowl and serve. Bits of chopped turkey meat may be added to each bowl as served. Serves 8.

Turkey

George Washington Ate Here

Chapter 3

Unique Cherry Soup

Cherries are not only for desserts. Try using them in soups and salads. If you are into drying fruit, late spring is the time to dry them for use this winter in any recipe that calls for raisins.

The cherry is native to the temperate regions of the Northern Hemisphere. The Romans discovered cherries in Eastern Europe, where they are still useful and valued in cooking and wine making. There are hundreds of varieties of cherries but most are not commercially available, as many are light croppers and do not stand up to the rigors of transportation. The three types that we are used to seeing are sweet, sour or hybrid.

As the cherry season is short, it is a good idea to buy more fruit than you can use immediately and either freeze, dry or can the excess for use later. If you are freezing or drying them, it is a good idea to stone them, since the stones may cause an "off" flavor if left in. You can buy a special cherry stoner at most kitchen stores. This little instrument will save a great deal of time. Try this Black Cherry Soup for a treat any season.

Black Cherry Soup

1 1/2 cups pitted black cherries
1 tablespoon butter
1 medium onion, sliced thin
1 tablespoon flour
3 cups chicken stock
1 stick (2 inches) cinnamon
2 whole cloves
2 strips lemon peel
2 egg yolks
Dairy sour cream for garnish

Stone and quarter 16 cherries for a garnish. Stone and chop the rest of the cherries.

Melt the butter in a saucepan; add onions. Cook over low heat until onion is soft but not browned. Stir in the flour; cook for 1 minute. Stir in stock and bring to a boil. Remove from heat. Add the chopped cherries, cinnamon, cloves and lemon peel. Bring soup back to a boil; reduce heat and simmer 20 minutes.

Strain the soup through a sieve, pressing down to extract as much liquid as possible. In a bowl, lightly beat the egg yolks and work in about a half cup of the cherry liquid. Mix the contents of the bowl into the rest of soup. Gently heat soup, but do not boil. Cook and then chill for a cold soup or serve at room temperature, garnished with a swirl of sour cream and the quartered cherries. Serves 8.

Cherries

A Summer Soup

Chapter 3

Super Soups

Melons belong to the cucumber family, and have been cultivated since the time of the Pharaohs. The rocks found on Mount Carmel are called "Elijah's melons." As the Bible relates the story, the owner of the land refused to supply food for the prophet, so in order to punish him, Elijah turned his melons into stone.

During the Renaissance, Ronsard praised the melon in his odes; Montaigne was fond of them; and in 1583, the dean of the College of Doctors in Lyon published a treatise on melons, in which he outlined 50 different ways to eat them. Some of the most common uses were in fritters, soups, compotes and relishes.

This chilled soup recipe will refresh you on a hot day. Use the ripest melons you can find, and substitute other varieties if you can't find just these melons.

Chilled Melon Soup

1 medium cantaloupe (2 cups cubed)

1 medium honeydew (3 cups cubed)

2 cups orange juice

Juice of 1 lime

Juice of 1 lemon

1 spice bundle: 2 cloves, 2 allspice,
   1 stick cinnamon

2 tablespoons honey

1 cup light cream

This soup can be made 2 days in advance. Just before serving, whisk in cream. Serve the soup in chilled bowls garnished with a dab of sour cream and a sprig of mint. Makes 6 servings.

Peel, seed and dice the melons. In a large saucepan, combine the melon pieces with juices. Combine spices in a cheesecloth bag; add to the melon mixture. Simmer over medium heat for 10 to 15 minutes. When the melon is very soft, remove from heat; cool. Discard the spice bundle and puree the soup. Chill in the refrigerator until ready to serve.

Cantaloupe

LET'S LEARN ABOUT PEAS

Gardeners impatiently await fresh peas, the first of the springtime vegetables to ripen, usually arriving during the first three weeks of June.

The Norse believed that the pea was sent by Thor the Thunder god to punish man. Thor sent flying dragons to scatter peas in wells, so they would rot and foul the water. Some peas, however, fell in fields and grew and the humans were so thankful they dedicated the new vegetable to Thor and only ate peas on Thursday, his day.

Catherine de Medici is credited with popularizing the petit pois. By the 17th century, fresh peas had become a cult food. In 1696, Madame de Maintenon called a conference that lasted four days where the princes discussed their love of peas.

They did not realize they were enjoying a highly nutritious vegetable: one cup of peas provides 458 milligrams potassium, 168 milligrams phosphorus and 903 units of vitamin A—not to mention the exercise required to shuck them.

The pea family is a single species, but there are hundreds of varieties. The major types we enjoy today are:

•Shell peas. These are mature peas that are eaten after the pod has been discarded.

•Snap peas. These are a recent addition to the American market. Snap peas look like miniature shell peas. They are sweet and tender and enjoyed, pod and all.

•Snow peas. These are immature peas that are eaten along with the flat pod. They were popularized by the Chinese, and are now widely grown in America.

One of the great soups for summer was invented by Chef Louis Diat for the opening of the Ritz- Carlton Hotel in New York. He flavored his new soup with fresh green peas. Diat had grown up in a village near Vichy in central France—thus the soup's name, vichyssoise.

SWEET PEAS VICHYSSOISE

1 pound fresh peas (2 1/2 cups shelled)

2 leeks (enough to make 3/4 cup chopped)

3 tablespoons butter

1 medium potato, peeled and diced

4 cups chicken stock

1 bouquet garni

1 cup light cream

Salt and black pepper

1 cup heavy cream

Fresh mint leaves

Cook 1/2 cup fresh peas in boiling, salted water for about 4 minutes. Drain and refresh under cold water; set aside. Chop the leeks and

Peas

Sweet Peas Vichyssoise (cont.)

Chapter 3

Super Soups

add to a large saucepan in which the butter has been melted. Cook until soft. Add the potato, chicken stock, bouquet garni and light cream. Simmer for 20 minutes or until the potatoes are tender. Add 2 cups peas and simmer for 5 minutes or until tender. Remove the bouquet garni and puree the soup. Season with salt and pepper. Remove from heat and cool. When cool, refrigerate until cold. Before serving, stir in the heavy cream. Sprinkle with chopped mint and the reserved chilled peas. Serves 6.

Peas

Fresh Sorrel Soup

Sorrel is savored more in France than in any other country.

In 1699, the English physician Sir Joseph Lister, on an official mission to France, was surprised to find how abundantly it was cultivated in the region of Paris, where whole acres were devoted to its growth. Lister found it to be healthful for a person and a good substitute for lemon in the treatment of scurvy and its related afflictions. Henry VIII enjoyed sorrel and had it used in salads and as cooking greens. In 1807, it was common in England, but by 1874 it had fallen from favor mainly because it had become popular in Ireland with the peasantry.

Sorrel is a member of the buckwheat family. It looks like young spinach with broad, bright green leaves on a single stem, tapering to a rounded point at the end. The similarities stop there, however, for the flavor is acidic, like lemon.

Fresh sorrel should be available in May and into summer and is usually expensive, so you may wish to grow your own. Seeds are available through garden shops, and greenhouses sometimes stock the French sorrel plants.

Fresh sorrel leaves can be used in a salad. Generally only a few leaves are added because this lemony herb goes a long way. More often, it is cooked in soups and sauces. One of the most popular uses is in a soup called schav, made with sorrel instead of beets. It was invented by the Jews of Eastern Europe. Today, it is enjoyed around the world.

Chilled Sorrel Soup (Schav)

1 pound fresh sorrel

2 medium potatoes, peeled, and cubed

1 leek

3 tablespoons butter

Salt and black pepper

2 cups water

2 cups chicken stock

1 tablespoon sugar

1 cup heavy cream

Lemon juice to taste

1 cup dairy sour cream

Green onions, chopped

Stem and wash the sorrel; cut into strips.

Peel and cube the potatoes into 1/2-inch dice. Wash the leek thoroughly; discard root and dark green leaves. Cut in half; finely chop.

Melt the butter in a large saucepan; cook the leek for 2 minutes over medium heat. Add the sorrel strips and potatoes and cook for 5 minutes. Add stock, water, salt, pepper and sugar. Simmer for 15 to 20 minutes. Puree the solids and gradually add the liquid. Transfer to a bowl and stir in the cream. Refrigerate for at least 1 hour. Just before serving, add lemon juice, plus more sugar and salt, if needed. Serve in chilled bowls with a dollop of sour cream. Garnish each with chopped green onions. Serves 8.

Pepper Pot

A Super Stew

Chapter 3

Super Soups

From a historian's point of view, American cooking is a newcomer.

Still, in a little more than 350 years, we've come a long way, establishing a cuisine of which we can be proud. We have borrowed from the classic dishes of Europe to the comic-strip world of the Dagwood sandwich, and we have incorporated the best of both into a rich and fascinating food heritage that includes tradition and modern technology.

Classic regional dishes make up the flavor of American cooking. To name a few, I would have to include strawberry shortcake, potato salad, fried chicken, apple pie and a casserole of some type.

One of the first and still most popular vegetables in America is corn, and one of my favorite recipes for using corn is Corn Stew. The original recipe probably would not resemble this one, but this one is good.

Corn Stew

4 tablespoons butter, divided

1 large onion, minced

1 green pepper, chopped

2 cups tomatoes, peeled and
  seeded, or 1 can (16 ounces), drained

2 pounds ground beef or chicken breast,
  skinned, boned and cubed

1/2 teaspoon cumin

1/2 teaspoon marjoram

3 tablespoons sugar, divided

1 teaspoon salt

1/4 teaspoon fresh ground pepper

1/2 cup raisins, soaked in water

12 stuffed green olives, sliced

3 hard-cooked eggs, sliced

3 cups frozen corn, thawed, or canned
  corn (white if possible)

1/4 cup flour

1 cup milk

6 eggs

In a large oven-proof skillet or casserole, melt 2 tablespoons of the butter. Add the onions and peppers; saute until wilted. Add the tomatoes; simmer for a few minutes. Add the meat and cook, stirring, until no longer pink. Add cumin, marjoram, 1 tablespoon sugar, salt and pepper; mix well. Stir in the raisins and olives. Remove from heat; layer sliced, hard-cooked eggs over mixture.

In a saucepan, melt the remaining butter; add the corn, 1 tablespoon sugar and salt to taste. Mix flour with the milk; add to corn, stirring and cooking until thickened. Cool slightly; add eggs, one at a time, stirring well after each.

Pour the corn mixture over meat and sprinkle with the remaining sugar. Bake at 350 degrees for 50 to 60 minutes, until puffed and golden brown. Serves 8.

Corn

A Swedish Specialty

Chapter

3

Super Soups

When autumn arrives in Sweden, the custom of serving a hot soup is observed. The most "Swedish" of soups—pea soup—is included on many menus every Thursday throughout autumn and winter.

This pea soup is made from dried yellow peas boiled for a long time with lightly salted pork. I found that this pork is really what we call ham shoulder. Thyme and marjoram give the soup a special flavor.

This thick pea soup with pork is really a meal in itself. It is traditionally followed with thin pancakes and jam—lingonberry, of course—and sour cream or creme fraiche.

Swedish Pea Soup with Pork

1 pound dry yellow peas

1 tablespoon salt

1 onion, sliced

1 pound lightly salted pork or ham

1/2 teaspoon thyme

1/2 teaspoon marjoram

Soak the peas in enough salted water to cover for 12 hours or overnight; drain. Place the pork or ham in a large soup pot; cover with water and add peas. Bring to a boil and skim. Add the onion. Cover and simmer for at least 1 1/2 hours or until the peas are soft and the meat is tender. (At altitude, this may take an additional hour.) Remove the meat and keep warm. Add the thyme and marjoram and keep hot until ready to serve. Cut the meat into cubes or slices. If meat is cubed, put the cubes into the soup. Or serve the meat sliced on a separate plate with a dab of mustard. This recipe serves 6 to 8.

Pig

JAMBALAYA

CHAPTER 3

Super Soups

Many authorities trace the origin of rice to India, but records as early as 2800 B.C. mentioned it when a Chinese emperor established a ceremonial for rice planting.

In the Middle Ages, rice was brought to Southern Europe and was introduced from there to America in 1694 when a sea captain traded some seeds to the governor of Charleston, S.C., for ship repairs.

Rice appears in many legends and has always been associated with fertility, which is still evident today in the tradition of throwing rice at weddings.

From the cook's point of view, rice is cheap, available and keeps for a long time. It is simple to prepare, having no strong flavor of its own. Thus it forms the basis of many different dishes, both sweet and savory.

Rice has been grown in the south for hundreds of years and is today still part of many Creole dishes. This version of Jambalaya combines Spanish and West African cooking. It is based on cold cooked rice and can be made with leftover chicken, ham, veal or sausage instead of prawns and bacon.

JAMBALAYA

3 ounces bacon, diced

1/2 cup chopped green onions

1 tablespoon flour

1 can (14 ounces) peeled
tomatoes, chopped

1 cup cold, cooked long-grain rice

1 cup prawns, boiled, peeled and deveined

Salt and pepper

1/8 teaspoon cayenne

2 tablespoons minced parsley

Cook the bacon in a large skillet over medium heat until fat begins to run. Add chopped onions and cook until golden. Stir in the flour and then the tomatoes with juices.

Add a little more water. Cook and stir over medium heat until thickened. When the mixture boils, stir in rice and prawns. Reduce heat to low and cook for 10 minutes, stirring occasionally. Season with salt, pepper and cayenne. Sprinkle with parsley and serve hot. Makes 4 servings. Serve with green salad.

Porridge

Cassoulet

With the freezing wind of winter, it is time to choose a real classic dish. The Cassoulet is a famous stew of white beans from the southwest of France. It takes its name from the pot in which it used to be cooked. Three towns claim to be the source of a true cassoulet. Whether it comes from Carcassone, Toulouse or Castelnaudary or any of the larger towns, each village, or for that matter, each chef or home cook, has a unique version.

In general, the beans are flavored with large sausages, and the dish will contain goose or duck, one meat (usually pork), and pork rind. Most of the time, all of the ingredients are included, but not required. The pork rind gives some gelatinous texture in addition to flavoring the dish. If possible, the dish should be cooked ahead of time and reheated, as it keeps several days in the refrigerator.

In this recipe, the roast pork and duck are combined at the last to retain a crisper meat. In the classic dish, all of the cooked meats are combined with the beans in a large, heavy casserole, topped with bread crumbs and baked until crisp. Both are good and the choice is a personal matter.

Cassoulet

2 pounds small dried white beans

1 1/4 pounds small, smoked pork butt

3 whole onions

2 large carrots

2 ribs celery

3 quarts water, plus 1 cup water

Bouquet garni (including 3 bay leaves, 12 whole cloves, 1 teaspoon dried thyme tied in a piece of cheesecloth)

1 tablespoon salt

Duck and pork roasts

Wash and pick over beans. Place in a heavy pot. Remove any rind from the pork butt; cut off the skin around the meat. Add the pork butt, whole onions, whole carrots and celery stalks. Add pork rind, water and bouquet garni along with the salt. Cover and simmer for 1 hour and 15 minutes. While the beans are cooking, roast the duck and the pork.

Roast Duck and Pork

1 pork shoulder blade roast (4 pounds) with some of the shoulder blade left in

4 cloves garlic, cut into slivers

1 duck, approximately 4 1/2 pounds

1/2 teaspoon salt

1/4 teaspoon pepper

1 pound seasoned sausage (chorizo will do)

1 cup water

1/4 cup fat from the roasts

Duck

CASSOULET (CONT.)

CHAPTER

3

Super Soups

2 cups fresh bread crumbs
1/4 cup chopped parsley

Pierce the pork roast; insert slivers of garlic here and there. Place the roast in a large roasting pan alongside the duck. Sprinkle with salt and pepper. Roast for 1 hour at 400 degrees. Pour off the fat. Turn the roast over and bake for another hour at 375 degrees.

The beans will be cooked after simmering for 1 hour and 15 minutes. Remove from heat and remove the pork butt, vegetables and pork rind; discard bouquet garni. Chop the cooked onions, carrots and celery coarse. Cut the pork rind into 1/4-inch pieces, and the pork butt into 1-inch pieces. Put all remaining ingredients back into the pot with the beans. Add the sausage in one piece or cut in half. Heat and simmer partially covered for 25 minutes.

Remove the pork roast and duck from the oven. Pour off all the fat from the pan; save. Add a cup of water to the pan and scrape any bits loose. Strain and save. Cut the duck into eight pieces (the two legs and two sides of the breast, cut into two pieces); cut the roast into slices. Place the meat and duck in the pan and keep warm. Heat 1/4 cup of the fat in a skillet and add bread crumbs. Heat and add the parsley; set aside.

Remove the sausage and cut into 3/4-inch slices. In another casserole, arrange the pieces of duck, pork and sausage. Layer with the cooked beans. Cover the top with the bread-crumb mixture. Drizzle some of the fat over the top. Bake for 45 minutes to an hour at 375 degrees. Serve hot from the pot. Dribble some of the reserved juices from the pan over each serving. Serves 8 to 10.

Duck

Cheers for Chowder

Clam chowder is a thick, appetite-satisfying soup, originally a specialty of New England. The original recipe goes back to the early settlers who had to make do with whatever food was available. Since fish and shellfish were plentiful, they were used from the beginning in all the old regional recipes.

Clam chowder fanciers are divided into two factions: New Englanders insist upon milk or cream and potatoes, while New Yorkers and many others prefer Manhattan chowder, which includes tomatoes among its ingredients. In Maine, a bill was once introduced in the state legislature to outlaw forever the mixing of clams and tomatoes. To try and keep peace among the factions, I have a recipe that should please most everyone.

All-American Clam Chowder

6 slices bacon or 3 1/2 ounces salt pork diced (New England recipes insist this must be salt pork)

2 onions, chopped

1 green pepper, in slivers

1/4 teaspoon parsley

1/4 teaspoon tarragon

1/4 teaspoon thyme

3 cups chicken or clam broth

8 ounces minced clams, drained, reserving juice

2 small potatoes, peeled and diced

2 medium tomatoes, peeled and diced

1 cup celery, sliced

Salt and cayenne pepper

4 tablespoons sour cream

2 egg yolks

Pinch of white pepper, optional

In a heavy saucepan, saute the bacon with the onions, green pepper and herbs. Cook over medium heat until the bacon is browned. Add the broth and clam liquid along with the potato, tomato and celery. Cook over low heat about 30 minutes or until the vegetables are tender. Add the clams and season to taste with the salt and cayenne. Combine the sour cream with the egg yolks and mix well. Stir into the chowder. Taste to see if you need the pinch of white pepper. Serve hot at once to 6 hungry guests.

Clam

A Sweet Corn Soup

Chapter 3

Super Soups

In the early 1900s, picture postcards featured a farmer balancing himself on a single ear of corn so big it filled his horsedrawn wagon. He was shown chopping off corn kernels with a pickax.

In those days, fresh corn lovers were limited to two indigenous types of corn known as dent and flint, bred for meal and fodder. Now, we can indulge in corn bred for sweetness and creaminess. Whereas Labor Day once meant the end of the affair, now corn lovers can feast on corn through the fall, savoring the ripeness of late bloomers.

In August, the corn is the sweetest, when corn lovers attack the tightly wrapped green-husked cobs with lakes of butter. This is the time to cut kernels from the cob and squeeze out the milky interiors so they may lend sweetening and thickening powers to companion foods.

The early colonists learned to use corn from the Indians of the West and East. They were taught to cut kernels from new corn to make succotash with new beans and other vegetables. They also learned to grate green corn and add it to their recipes for soups, puddings, fritters and griddlecakes.

This recipe for corn and cucumber soup is good served cold on a hot day.

Sweet Corn and Cucumber Soup

2 tablespoons butter

2 green onions, chopped with tops

4 cups cucumbers, peeled and sliced

6 cups chicken broth

3 cups fresh corn kernels

1 cup plain yogurt

Salt and pepper to taste

Garnish with chopped chives

Melt the butter in a large kettle. Add the onions and saute. Add the cucumbers and chicken broth; simmer for 15 minutes. Add all but 1/2 cup of the corn; simmer for 5 minutes more. Remove from heat and puree in a processor or blender. Add up to 1 cup of the yogurt, depending on the thickness desired. Season with salt and pepper. Chill 2 hours. Serve in chilled bowls. Garnish with a sprinkle of the remaining corn kernels and chopped chives. Serves 6 to 8.

Cucumber

The Terrific Tomato

The tomato is actually a fruit, but is used as one of our most versatile and popular vegetables. It may be cooked in soups and sauces, or grilled, baked or fried. I feel it is best eaten raw in salads and sandwiches. Wherever used, the tomato contributes flavor and goodness to a meal.

The tomato was discovered by the Spanish in South America and soon taken back to Spain, where it flourished in the hot, sunny climate. In a few years it reached North Africa and Italy, where it was known as "pom di Mori." It quickly traveled to southern France and was known as "pomme d'amour." By the middle of the 16th century it was common in England, where both the red and yellow varieties were equally used.

Tomatoes now grow all over the world and are available throughout the year. In tropical and temperate climates they are grown outside, but are successfully grown in northern countries in greenhouses.

It is fairly easy to grow your own, either in a sunny spot in your yard or in pots. You have an extensive range of plants from which to choose. Cherry tomatoes which go nicely in salads, either whole or cut into halves; yellow tomatoes boast a sweet flavor and are most decorative because of their color; the ornamental tomatoes include those that are pear-shaped, a cherry type that grows in clusters like grapes, and a new one I discovered is a stuffing tomato that is hollow like a bell pepper.

Later in the summer tomatoes are quite inexpensive and it is the best time to make chutney and sauces for canning. Purees may be frozen and used throughout the year. Raw tomatoes are eaten by themselves, mixed with other vegetables or combined with eggs, cheese or chicken. The French enjoy serving them sliced, with a simple herb vinaigrette dressing. The Italians enjoy them sliced with mozzarella cheese and chopped fresh basil, sprinkled with olive oil and freshly ground pepper.

A summertime favorite of mine is an uncooked Spanish soup, served ice cold, called gazpacho.

Gazpacho

1 small clove garlic
6 large tomatoes, peeled and chopped
1 Spanish onion, chopped
1 large green pepper, chopped
1 cucumber, peeled, seeded and chopped

6 tablespoons olive oil
4 tablespoons lemon juice
1 cup tomato juice, chilled
1/2 cup chicken stock
Salt and cayenne pepper to taste

Blend the garlic with 4 of the tomatoes in a blender or food processor. Add half the

Tomato

CHAPTER 3

Super Soups

chopped onion, one-fourth of the pepper and half of the cubed cucumber. Process again. Strain into a soup tureen and chill.

Just before serving, blend the olive oil and lemon juice with the chilled tomato juice and chicken stock. Season with salt and cayenne pepper.

Stir the remainder of the vegetables into the chilled mixture in a tureen or serve the remaining vegetables from small bowls, to be added by each guest to his soup. Serve with garlic croutons. This recipe will serve 4 persons but doubles easily.

Chilled Tomato Soup

    9 cups tomato juice
    1/4 cup plus 2 tablespoons tomato puree
    Zest of two limes
    1/4 cup plus 2 tablespoons lime juice
    6 small green onions, minced
    1 1/2 teaspoons sugar
    1 teaspoon salt
    1 1/2 teaspoons curry powder
    3/4 teaspoon ground thyme
    3 dashes Tabasco
    2 cups dairy sour cream
    Fresh parsley, chopped

Combine in a large pitcher, the tomato juice, tomato puree, lime zest and juice, onions, sugar, salt, curry powder, thyme, and Tabasco sauce; stir well. Chill for 4 to 6 hours. Just before serving, whisk in sour cream and garnish with chopped parsley.

Tomato

CHAPTER 4

Poultry & Fowl

Goose

Rooster

Hen

Tur-key

THE FIRST THANKSGIVING

CHAPTER 4

Poultry & Fowl

There is no exact record of the bill of fare for the famous first harvest festival of 1621, often referred to as the "First Thanksgiving."

The event is mentioned in but two quotes—one from William Bradley in his Of Plymouth Plantation and the other in a letter written by Edward Winslow. We have no specific date for the three-day celebration, but we do know it was between Sept. 21, when the Shallop returned from Massachusetts Bay, and the arrival of the Fortune with new settlers Nov. 9.

There were about 140 people at the harvest celebration: 90 Indian men and some 50 Pilgrims. Only four adult women survived the first winter: Elizabeth Hopkins, Elinore Billington, Mary Brewster and Susanna White. They probably oversaw the cooking and preparations, with the help of some children and servants.

We do know the feast included cod, sea bass, wild fowl (such as ducks, geese, turkeys and swans), cornmeal and probably rye, and five deer brought by the Indians, but not cooked for the feast.

The meats were roasted or boiled English fashion, and the fish was boiled—since the Indians had not yet taught the new arrivals to grill. The herbs were either boiled along with the meats as "sauce," or used in "sallets." "Sallet" was a vegetable dish either cooked or raw, and either simple or compound (that is made from one ingredient or several). The popularity of sallet was not great at this time.

The Pilgrims dined on a number of native and English fruits and herbs. Many were found wild; others were cultivated. Native plants known were walnuts, chestnuts, grapes, plums, gooseberries, raspberries, wild cherries, wild strawberries, watercress, beans, peas, pumpkins, squash, currants, Jerusalem artichokes, cranberries and wild onions. English native plants included parsnips, carrots, turnips, onions, cabbage, melons, radishes, beets and lettuce. Not all of these were available at first. The pea crop had failed, but the barley survived and provided colonists with malt for beer. Beer was served to both adults and children.

No animals other than two dogs are mentioned as having come on the Mayflower. It is reasonable to assume there were chickens and possibly cats, goats (for milk) and pigs. It is unlikely any of the livestock was slaughtered because colonists were trying to build their stock. There is a good chance eggs and goat milk were available.

This recipe for Roast Fowl is from the original menu. All goose, swan, duck and turkey were cooked in this fashion.

Goose

Plymouth Roast Fowl

Chapter

4

Poultry & Fowl

Plymouth Roast Fowl

1 10-pound bird

1 cup cooked oats

3 large onions

2 teaspoons thyme

3/4 cup water

2 teaspoons sage

1 teaspoon marjoram

Salt and pepper

1/4 cup vinegar

Remove the giblets and neck from the fowl and wash inside and out, drying thoroughly. Stuff the body cavity loosely with cooked oats and onions. Place on a rack in a large roasting pan and roast uncovered for 2 hours. Remove the fowl from oven and draw off fat. Return to oven and cook for another hour.

To make sauce, take some of the drippings from the fowl with some of the oats and onions. Mix well with thyme, water, sage, marjoram, salt and pepper. Stir in vinegar and bring to a boil. Place fowl on a serving dish; drench with sauce and serve. Serves 8 to 10 people.

Goose

A Vote For Burgoo

CHAPTER 4

Poultry & Fowl

These days politicians try to garner votes by inviting anyone who can afford it to join them at any number of luncheons and dinners, affairs that cost anywhere from $25 to $2,500 to attend.

The policy of plying potential voters with food and drink was practiced by politicians from Washington's time onward. This type of wheeling and dealing campaigning reached its zenith in the campaign of 1840 when William Henry Harrison was running for president. His lieutenants were sent throughout the territory to wine and dine the populace. The first step was to erect a log cabin (the symbol of his campaign), then invite all eligible voters to a feast of cornbread, cheese and hard cider. This type of political barbecue increased in popularity, with the largest being held in Wheeling, W.V., where 30,000 hungry voters were served 360 hams, 20 calves, 25 sheep, 1,500 pounds of beef, 8,000 pounds of bread and 4,500 pies. As the crowds increased, a mass quantity type of food was needed. Harrison quickly learned that the ideal dish to serve was Burgoo, the master election dish, as it was expandable to the size of the crowd. This stew could use anything on hand. The purists insisted that the most important ingredient be squirrel. Since I am not this "pure," I offer a version that substitutes chicken for squirrel.

Burgoo

1 3-pound chicken, cut up

2 pounds beef shank, cross cut

12 cups water

1 tablespoon salt

1/4 teaspoon pepper

6 slices bacon

2 cans (28 ounces each) tomatoes, chopped

2 cups cubed potatoes

2 cups chopped carrots

1 cup chopped onion

1 cup chopped celery

1 cup chopped green pepper

2 tablespoons brown sugar

1/4 teaspoon crushed dried red pepper

4 whole cloves

1 bay leaf

1 clove garlic, minced

4 ears corn

2 cans or 4 cups cooked butter beans

1 cup okra, sliced if large

2/3 cup flour

1/2 cup chopped parsley

In a 12-quart pot, combine the chicken, beef, water, salt and pepper. Cover and cook until meat is tender. Remove chicken and beef from the pot; save broth. Remove meat from

Squirrel

Burgoo (cont.)

Chapter 4

Poultry & Fowl

bones; discard skin and bones. Cube beef and chicken; set aside.

In a frying pan cook bacon crisp; drain, reserving grease. To the reserved broth, add the beef, undrained tomatoes, potatoes, carrots, onions, celery, green pepper, sugar, red pepper, cloves, bay leaf and garlic. Cover and simmer for one hour, stirring often. Remove cloves and bay leaf. Cut corn from cob with a knife and scrape cob. Add the corn, cubed chicken, beans and okra to the pot and simmer 20 minutes. Blend bacon dripping with flour; stir in. Cook and stir until stew is thick. Taste for seasoning, adding salt if needed. Serve in bowls garnished with parsley and crumbled bacon. Serves 20 hungry voters.

Squirrel

PERFECT ROAST CHICKEN

CHAPTER 4

Poultry & Fowl

Crisp and golden-skinned, with juicy and flavorsome flesh, is how a roast chicken should be cooked.

It was not until the 16th century that Henry VI of France declared that a chicken in the pot every Sunday should be the right of every Frenchman. Centuries later in America, our politicians proclaimed the same right.

A dish that I learned about in France is a tender roast chicken with a sharp, clear flavor of lemon juice and the rich savor of saffron, served with creamy mushroom sauce. Though this dish is typically French in feeling, it has a strong hint of its African heritage, for the Arabs have used lemon and saffron with chicken for centuries. This makes a wonderful addition to your store of chicken recipes for that special Sunday dinner.

ROAST CHICKEN WITH LEMON AND SAFFRON

3 1/2-pound roasting chicken

Salt and black pepper

6 tablespoons butter

1/2 teaspoon powdered (or strands) saffron

1 small clove garlic, minced

Juice of 1/2 lemon

1 tablespoon flour

Sauce

Watercress for garnish

Let the chicken come to room temperature. Heat oven to 425 degrees. Wipe chicken clean both inside and out; pat dry. Season the inside with salt and pepper.

Put butter in a bowl and, with a wooden spoon, work in the saffron, garlic and lemon juice. Season with salt and pepper. Put half of the seasoned butter into the cavity of the bird. Truss the chicken. Spread the remaining butter over the breast and thighs. Season with salt and pepper.

Lay the chicken on its side in a roasting pan and roast for 20 minutes at 425 degrees or until slightly browned. Turn the chicken to the other side and roast for another 15 minutes. Remove chicken from oven; turn on its back. Reduce heat to 350 degrees. Sift flour over the breast. Dribble 3 or 4 tablespoons hot water over it and roast for another 30 to 35 minutes at 350 degrees or longer, if necessary, basting several times with juices in the pan.

To test if the chicken is done, push a skewer into the thickest part of the inside of the leg; if the juices run clear, it should be done. The juices in the cavity should also be clear. While the chicken is roasting, make the sauce.

Cock

PERFECT ROAST CHICKEN (CONT.)

CHAPTER 4

Poultry & Fowl

SAUCE

4 tablespoons butter

1/2 cup sliced fresh mushrooms

2 egg yolks

1/2 cup heavy cream

Zest of 1/2 lemon

Juice of 1/2 lemon

4 teaspoons sugar

6 tablespoons dry white wine

Salt and black pepper

Melt butter in a saucepan; lightly saute sliced mushrooms. Remove mushrooms with a slotted spoon; set aside. In a bowl, place egg yolks with the cream, lemon zest, lemon juice and sauteed mushrooms; mix lightly.

In a small heavy pan, place sugar; melt over medium heat. Let sugar boil to a rich caramel color. Hold pan at arms' length and add 2 tablespoons hot water. Over low heat, let it cook until mixture is like syrup. Stir syrup into egg-cream-mushroom mixture.

Remove the trussing from chicken and place on a warm platter. Pour juices into roasting pan, add wine, and place over high heat; bring to a boil, stirring and scraping the pan to dislodge any bits. Boil until reduced by half.

To finish sauce, place cream mixture into the top of a double boiler, with boiling water underneath. Drain juices from roasting pan into cream; whisk for about 5 minutes or until lightly thickened. Do not allow sauce to boil or it will curdle. Season with salt and pepper and pour into a heated sauceboat. Serve immediately with roast chicken that has been garnished with a few sprigs of watercress. Serves 4.

Cock

George Washington Ate Here

Chapter 4

Chicken Marengo

Tomatoes are America's favorite homegrown vegetable. The U.S. Department of Agriculture confirms it is the first choice of more than 80 percent of American home gardeners.

The tomato has not always been as well loved. It was not even considered a food until the early 1800s, and then was grown as a British greenhouse novelty. It was shunned in Europe for cooking because it was considered to be a dangerous aphrodisiac. In fact, until 100 years ago, its nickname was the "love apple." In 1860, the readers of the women's magazine Godey's Lady's Book were warned not to serve tomatoes unless they were cooked for "three hours before eating."

The tomato made its debut in European cuisine in a dish called Chicken Marengo. According to culinary history, Napoleon's chef was faced with the task of providing a superb meal for his general on the battlefield during the Battle of Marengo at Piedmont. He had assembled all the basic ingredients but had only one cooking pot, so he blended everything together and created a dish that has won universal acclaim—Chicken Marengo.

Chicken Marengo

8 portions of chicken

Seasoned flour to coat

8 tablespoons butter

2 tablespoons vegetable oil

16 small white onions

2 cloves garlic, minced

1 1/2 cups dry white wine

2 pounds tomatoes, peeled, seeded and chopped

2 bay leaves

2 cups chicken broth

2 tablespoons tomato paste

1 pound button mushrooms

12 to 15 pitted ripe olives

Parsley for garnish

Coat chicken pieces with the seasoned flour. Heat the butter and oil in a large kettle. Add chicken and onions. Saute gently until golden brown, about 10 minutes. Add the garlic and cook for another 2 or 3 minutes. Pour in the wine; increase the heat. Reduce sauce to about half.

Stir in tomatoes, bay leaf, broth and tomato paste. Cover and simmer for 20 minutes. Trim stems of the mushrooms and add with the olives. Continue to simmer, uncovered, for about 10 minutes, until any excess liquid has evaporated. Remove bay leaves. Sprinkle with chopped parsley and serve at once. Serves 8.

Hen Pecking

Country Captain

Chapter 4

Poultry & Fowl

The origin of Country Captain has never really been ascertained. Almost any good Georgia cook will claim it came to Georgia many years ago from India via England. I found it listed in a cookbook published in 1896 in Charleston, S.C.

It is known as a favorite dish of presidents and generals. When President Franklin Delano Roosevelt visited Warm Springs, he requested the dish. It was always prepared for him when in Georgia by members of his staff.

One of the famous hostesses of Georgia thought enough of the dish she served it to President Roosevelt and some of his distinguished guests on several occasions in Warm Springs.

A story about the dish concerns Gen. George Patton. At one time, when he was enroute through Georgia and could spend only a few hours in Columbus, he wired ahead: "If you can't give me a party and have Country Captain, put some in a bucket and bring it to the train."

When Dwight Eisenhower was commanding in Europe during and after the war, he had it served on several occasions to friends and guests.

One gala of note was a Halloween party given by Mamie for the staff. It was one of the most interesting parties ever seen in the dignified setting of the White House. The main dish served was Country Captain.

Country Captain

Flour

Salt and pepper, as desired

10 to 12 pieces chicken, skinned

2 to 3 tablespoons oil

2 onions, finely chopped

1 large green pepper, chopped

1/2 pound fresh mushrooms, sliced

1 clove garlic, minced

1 teaspoon salt

1/2 teaspoon white pepper

2 teaspoons curry powder

2 cans (15 ounces each) tomatoes

1 teaspoon chopped parsley

1/2 teaspoon thyme

4 ounces slivered almonds

1/2 cup currants

In a paper bag, mix the flour with salt and pepper, as desired. Coat chicken pieces with flour mixture. Heat oil in a large skillet and brown chicken on all sides; remove to a baking pan and keep warm.

Drain some of the drippings from the skillet; add onions, green pepper, mushrooms and garlic. Cook slowly, stirring constantly. Season with 1 teaspoon salt, 1/2 teaspoon

Rooster

Country Captain (cont.)

Chapter 4

Poultry & Fowl

white pepper and curry powder. Stir in tomatoes, parsley and thyme. Heat thoroughly and then pour over the chicken. Be sure sauce covers the chicken. Cover the pan and bake at 350 degrees for 45 minutes. Meanwhile, toast the almonds.

Cook 2 cups of rice and have ready to serve. When ready to serve, place chicken in center of a platter and surround with rice. Add currants to sauce and heat. When sauce is hot, pour it over the chicken. Garnish with toasted almonds and chopped parsley. Makes 8 servings.

Rooster

POMEGRANATE CHICKEN

CHAPTER 4

Poultry & Fowl

The name "pomegranate" comes from the Latin pomoum, "apple," and granatum, "full of seeds." In Greek mythology, the pomegranate is responsible for winter. Persephone, daughter of the Harvest Goddess, Demeter, was abducted by Pluto to Hades. Enraged, her mother cursed the Earth, withering crops and killing cattle. After many entreaties from gods and men, Zeus gave Demeter leave to fetch her daughter back to Mount Olympus. Along the way, the maiden ate six pomegranate seeds, so from that time forward she was obliged to spend six months of each year in Hades. Demeter, rejoicing at her daughter's return, gave the world six months of spring and summer. When Persephone is absent, the mother's lament takes the form of autumn and winter.

The pomegranate fruit looks like a leathery red ball filled with ruby-colored seeds. In hot climates, its refreshing juice is an ideal thirst-quencher. Its flavor is tart, like cranberry; perfumed, like rose water; and refreshing as fresh-squeezed orange juice. The juice is only half of the pleasure, for the fleshy seeds can be delightful to chew. They can also be swallowed.

This recipe comes from the Caucasus, a mountainous region of southern Russia, where people commonly live to over 100.

CHICKEN WITH POMEGRANATE SAUCE

4 whole boneless chicken breasts

3 pomegranates

3/4 cup walnuts

1 small onion or 2 shallots

Flour for dredging

Salt and black pepper

3 tablespoons butter

Juice of 1 lemon

1 cup chicken stock

1/2 teaspoon ground cinnamon

Pinch of ground coriander

1/2 teaspoon sugar

Cut breasts in half; trim fat or sinew. Cut 2 pomegranates in half; press out juice. Break third pomegranate in half; extract whole seeds. You should have 2/3 cup juice, 1 cup seeds. Finely chop walnuts. Finely chop onion or shallots. Heat oven to 350 degrees.

Dredge chicken in a mixture of flour, salt, pepper. Heat butter in a large frying pan (not cast iron or aluminum). Lightly brown chicken. Transfer to baking dish. Lower heat; cook onion or shallots until tender, adding walnuts halfway through. Deglaze pan with lemon juice. Add pomegranate juice, stock, cinnamon, coriander, sugar, salt and pepper. Sauce should be balanced sweet-sour. Taste. If needed, add lemon juice. Reduce sauce to coating consistency.

Drain chicken juices into sauce. Pour over chicken; bake 15 minutes, or until cooked through. Sprinkle with pomegranate seeds. Serves 8.

Hen & Chicks

Chicken Paprika

Chapter 4

Poultry & Fowl

The first written record of paprika as we know it appears in letters that Chanca, Columbus' ship surgeon, wrote to the court surgeon of King Phillip of Spain. In them he describes "Indian pepper" growing in the New World, a spice which could prove medically useful. Although Chanca brought some of these interesting plants from America, for a long time paprika remained a botanical curiosity. By the end of the 16th century, a flourishing paprika culture had grown up in the Iberian peninsula. All these facts constitute solid evidence Columbus introduced paprika to Europe.

After the Italians introduced paprika to Italy, the Turks took the seeds from there to the Balkans, which was then part of the Ottoman domain. In the 16th century, the Turkish Empire included Bulgaria and most of Hungary. The Bulgarians have been known as the "Gardeners of Europe." Having learned to cultivate paprika from seeds given them by the Turks, many Bulgarian gardeners emigrated to Hungary during the 16th century, partly attracted by the more favorable soil and climate.

When a Hungarian says "paprika," it means only the ground spice, referred to as "red paprika." Green paprika refers to the green vegetable. There are two basic categories of paprika: those grown for eating fresh, cooked or marinated, and those destined to be dried, ground into powder and used as a condiment.

Paprika endured a slow climb to acceptance as a national treasure. It rose from the lowest classes—through the masses of fishermen and peasants—to the townspeople and gentry. The nobility were the last to acknowledge paprika. Eighteenth century records are full of recipes for pate and fish dishes calling for paprika.

In 1844, Chicken Paprikas appeared on the menu of the National Casino, the exclusive club of the Hungarian House of Lords. Here it was served to the beautiful and popular Queen Elizabeth (Franz Josef I's consort). The dish became her favorite each time she visited Hungary, until her assassination in 1860. Her love of the dish won over the Hungarian aristocracy to paprika, and "Paprika's Chicken" became one of the most popular dishes not only in Hungary, but also in the world.

This recipe is basically the same today as it was in 1844.

Chicken

CHICKEN PAPRIKA (CONT.)

Chapter 4

Poultry & Fowl

CHICKEN PAPRIKA

2 tablespoons lard

2 medium onions, peeled, and minced

3 pounds cut-up chicken, washed and dried

1 large ripe tomato, peeled, and cut into pieces

2 tablespoons paprika

1 teaspoon salt

1 green pepper, sliced

2 tablespoons dairy sour cream

1 tablespoon flour

2 tablespoons whipping cream

Melt the lard in a heavy pot with a tight-fitting lid. Add the onions and cook over low heat for 5 minutes. Do not brown. Add the chicken and tomato; cook, covered, for 10 minutes. Stir in the paprika. Add 1/2 cup water and salt. Cook, covered, over low heat for 30 minutes. Toward the end of the time, remove the lid and continue to cook to let the liquid evaporate. Let the chicken stew in its own fat and juices, taking care that it does not burn. Remove the chicken pieces. In a bowl, mix the sour cream with the flour and 1 teaspoon cold water. Stir into the pot and cook until it is smooth and of an even color. Add the green

pepper, replace the chicken pieces; taste for salt. Replace the lid and cook over low heat until the peppers are tender. Just before serving, whip in the whipping cream. In Hungary, more sour cream is spread on each piece of chicken when serving. Serves 8.

Chicken

Comfort Foods

Chapter 4

Poultry & Fowl

Ah, comfort foods! The bread pudding, chicken soup and other comfy, cozy foods of childhood are back, but with a difference. While they're just as comforting, they can be used as part of a lighter, healthier diet.

Modifying old-time favorite foods to make them part of a healthy eating plan is easier than you might think. Almost any recipe can be changed to reduce fat, cholesterol, sugar and sodium, or to add fiber.

Depending upon the recipe, an ingredient might be eliminated, reduced or replaced by a more wholesome ingredient. For example, adding oil and salt to the water to cook pasta is unnecessary if you stir it occasionally to prevent sticking and season the sauce with extra herbs and spices.

Sugar often can be cut by one-third to one-half in dessert recipes. The oil or margarine used for sauteing vegetables in skillet dishes can also be reduced, especially if you use a non-stick pan.

Many ingredients have healthful substitutes. Plain low-fat yogurt can replace sour cream in dressings, dips and some baked products. Doing so will reduce fat and cholesterol as well as trim calories. Try substituting skim or low-fat milk for whole milk in sauces, puddings and beverages; low-moisture, part-skim mozzarella cheese can replace Cheddar and other high-fat cheeses in casseroles and pasta dishes. Thicken soups and stews with ground oat flour rather than all-purpose flour. Ground oat flour can be made in the blender or food processor and stored, tightly covered, in the refrigerator for added convenience.

In recipes that call for ground beef, substitute ground turkey for all or part of the beef. Considerably lower in both fat and cholesterol, ground turkey is available in many supermarkets both fresh and frozen, usually in one-pound rolls. Because it is uncooked, it can be used just like ground beef in pizza toppings, spaghetti sauce, burgers, meatballs…even a new-fashioned meat loaf.

Spinach-Stuffed Turkey Meat Loaf has more than a reduced fat content going for it. Oats added to the meat mixture for easier shaping contribute the dietary fiber which was common in Grandma's day but often is lacking in today's diets.

Fiber has a number of health benefits. And, now, the results of two studies conducted by Northwestern University Medical School indicate that oats, a source of water-soluble fiber can actually help reduce blood cholesterol levels when eaten as part of a fat-modified diet. And lowering blood cholesterol levels potentially reduces the risk of heart attack.

Tur-key

Spinach-Stuffed Turkey Meat Loaf

Chapter 4

Poultry & Fowl

Spinach-Stuffed Turkey Meat Loaf

1 package (10 ounces) frozen chopped
   spinach, thawed and drained

1 cup coarsely chopped mushrooms

1/4 cup chopped onion

1 tablespoon margarine

1/2 cup shredded Swiss cheese, divided

1/4 cup grated Parmesan cheese

1 pound ground turkey

1/2 pound ground beef

3/4 cup oats (quick or old-fashioned),
   uncooked

1/2 cup milk

1 whole egg or egg white, beaten

1 teaspoon salt (optional)

1/4 teaspoon pepper

Heat oven to 375 degrees. Saute spinach, mushrooms and onion in margarine over medium heat 3 to 4 minutes. Stir in 1/4 cup Swiss cheese and Parmesan cheese. Combine turkey, ground beef, oats, milk, egg or egg white, salt and pepper; mix well.

Spoon two-thirds of the meat mixture lengthwise down center of pan; fill with spinach mixture. Top with remaining meat mixture to encase spinach filling. Bake 50 to 55 minutes. Sprinkle with remaining Swiss cheese; return to oven 1 to 2 minutes or until cheese is melted. Let stand 5 minutes before slicing. Serves 8.

Tur-key

A Lesson on Pears

Throughout history, the apple captured all the lead roles—except in Colonial America. During this time, the pear rivaled the apple in the use of wine, sauce, preserves and a type of hard cider. Today, this fruit is making a great comeback.

Presently, there are more than 300 varieties of apples, most of them developed during the 19th century. In France, a different pear is available almost every month of the year. Pears are grouped into two classes: the soft-fleshed European variety and the hard-fleshed Oriental. The soft-fleshed ones include the Comice, Bartlett and Anjou. The hard-fleshed type includes the Seckel and Asian.

Some of the varieties common in the United States are:

Comice (also called red pear): It is the aristocrat of pears with a bright red skin that covers a fine white flesh that is fragrant and pleasing. There are some green-skinned members of this family. It is good both for eating and for desserts.

Bartlett: In America, it is most popular and is the same as the Williams pear of Europe. It was brought to this country in the 18th century by a farmer named Brewer, but is named for his neighbor, Enoch Bartlett, a merchant who promoted it under his own name and later bought Brewer's orchard. Today, this fragrant and juicy pear is the most widely grown in the country. It has a yellow skin with a blush of red.

Anjou: This pear is named for a town in the Loire Valley in France. It is a large, plump fruit with a short neck and a yellow-green skin. Its flesh is smooth with a spicy aftertaste.

Bosc: This pear is recognized by its long, tapered neck with a russet skin. The Bosc is mildly acidic with a slightly grainy texture.

Seckel: This one usually arrives on the market during the first part of October, and is named for a farmer in Philadelphia who first grew it. This pear is small and long-necked with a russet or green-brown color. The flesh is crisp with a grainy texture. It is best for salads and canning and is excellent with poultry.

Asian: Round like an apple with a green-brown skin speckled with rust color, this pear's flesh is crisp and snappy with a somewhat bland flavor.

This recipe for duckling I ran into while attending the La Varenne School for Cooking in Paris.

Chapter 4 / Poultry & Fowl

Pear

RAGOUT OF DUCKLING WITH PEARS

CHAPTER 4

Poultry & Fowl

RAGOUT OF DUCKLING WITH PEARS

1 5-pound duckling

Salt and black pepper

4 underripe pears

4 tablespoons brown sugar

1 tablespoon butter

1/4 cup wine vinegar

1 cup duck or veal stock

1/2 teaspoon cornstarch

2 tablespoons Poire William or cognac

Cut the duck into quarters—2 leg sections and 2 breast-wing sections. Discard any lumps of fat. Season the pieces with salt and pepper. In a large skillet, add the duck pieces skin side down and cook over medium heat for 10 minutes, or until browned on all sides. Pour off any extra fat and continue to cook, with low heat, for another 20 minutes. Transfer the duck to a warm platter and discard all but 2 tablespoons of the fat.

Peel, halve and core the pears. Rub them with a little lemon juice to keep them from turning brown. Place the pears in the skillet and brown them with the brown sugar and butter. Cook over high heat until the sugar caramelizes. Add the vinegar and stir until the sugar and pan juices are dissolved. Add the stock and simmer for 10 minutes or until the pears are tender. Taste for salt and pepper.

To finish the dish, warm the duck in the sauce. Remove and arrange the duck and pears on a warm platter. Dissolve the cornstarch in the Poire or cognac and whisk it into the pan juices. Simmer the sauce for a few seconds, then pour it over the duck and pears. If you really want to make an impression, warm some of the Poire or cognac in a small saucepan and ignite it. Pour the flaming liquor over the platter as you present it. Serves 4.

Duckling

Harrison's Favorite Duck

William Henry Harrison was born in Charles City, Va., where his love of fine food and the importance of hospitality were nurtured. Later he moved to Vincennes, Ind., where he served as governor of the Northwest Territory.

His hospitality followed wherever his family lived. While governor of the territory, he was continually sending back to Philadelphia for coffee, sugar, tea, Madeira wine and rice. He was known as an excellent shot and spent occasional afternoons hunting for partridge, geese, ducks, deer and turkey.

Timothy Flint, writing of the Harrisons' home, describes the table as loaded with abundance and substantial good cheer, "especially with the different kinds of game." On his fine farm, he was known as a good gardener. In 1830 he wrote home: "I have an excellent garden with beans, peas, cabbages, cauliflower, celery and artichokes in abundance, and soon we shall have beets."

After being elected president, he traveled to Washington, D.C., Feb. 9, 1841. Mrs. Harrison did not accompany him because of ill health. The day of his inauguration was cold and stormy. After taking the oath of office, he proceeded to issue the longest inaugural address on record, one hour and 45 minutes. On the way back to the White House, he caught a severe cold and died of pneumonia in April 1841.

President Harrison did his own shopping in Washington, where he found the markets stocked abundant supplies of the finest game and fish. During his short term in office, he gave numerous parties that were hostessed by his daughter-in-law, Mrs. William Henry Harrison, Jr., widow of his eldest son.

Sunday dinner at the Harrison home was usually shared with at least 50 guests. Because of his love for wild or domestic duck, it was the most popular dish served for these dinners.

Roast Wild or Domestic Duck

2 2-pound wild ducks or 2 4- pound
    domestic ducks

1/2 lemon

White pepper and salt

2 oranges

1 clove garlic, bruised

1 cup red wine

Lump of butter (4 oz.)

1 cup orange juice

1/2 cup orange marmalade

Remove gizzards, hearts, livers and necks from the ducks. Wash fowl thoroughly inside and out. Rub half a lemon inside and out. Dry well with paper towel. Season inside with salt

Wild Duck

Harrison's Favorite Duck (cont.)

Chapter

4

Poultry & Fowl

and pepper. Cut oranges into quarters and stuff ducks with them. Add the bruised garlic and a small lump of butter. Tie up the duck and arrange on a rack. Brush with melted butter. Pour a little of the red wine into the roasting pan (save the rest for basting). Roast wild duck for 25 to 30 minutes at 450 degrees; domestic duck should be roasted at 350 degrees for 35 minutes per pound (2 1/2 to 3 hours for a 4- or 5-pound bird).

Baste occasionally with a mixture of orange juice and wine. Each time you baste, brush with melted butter. Turn on its breast for part of the time. Ten minutes before it is roasted, brush with the marmalade to glaze.

Wild Duck

Coq au Beaujolais

In France on Nov. 15 at precisely 10:01 a.m., the clock signals the official release of Beaujolais nouveau, the "new" Beaujolais. True oenophiles go to any lengths to be the first on the block to drink it. In past years, the wine has been chauffeured in a limo to Paris, jetted by Concorde to New York and parachuted into London.

The Beaujolais is a 45-mile expanse of rolling hills, two-lane roads and steepled villages between the distinguished wine districts of Burgundy and the Cote du Rhone. The wine is made from the gamay grape, a viti-cultural oddball that prospers in the region's stony soil. Some Beaujolais, particularly that from the villages of Brouilly, Morgon and Fleurie, is capable of extended bottle age. But the bulk is meant to be drunk the same year it is made.

This "new wine" is barely a wine at all, since only six weeks have elapsed since the grapes were picked, pressed, fermented, filtered and bottled. This is the infamous new Beaujolais, also called primeur. It is young stuff—purple in color, grapy in smell, light with alcohol, rough and fruity. The wine growers love it, as they can turn their inventory over in a few weeks which accounts for about a third of the bottles made in this region.

Coq au Beaujolais

1 chicken, 3 to 4 pounds

1 onion

2 carrots

2 sticks celery

1 clove garlic

1 tablespoon olive oil

1 bottle Beaujolais

Bouquet garni (bay leaf, thyme, parsley, peppercorns)

1/4 pound thick sliced bacon

Salt and pepper

2 tablespoons flour

1/2 pound pearl onions, for garnish

1/2 pound fresh mushrooms, for garnish

1/2 cup chopped parsley

Cut chicken into 8 pieces (legs, thighs, breasts, wings). Finely chop the onion, carrots, celery and garlic. Combine with the olive oil, wine and bouquet garni. Pour over the chicken and marinate overnight.

Drain chicken and save the marinade. Pat the chicken dry. Cut the bacon into bits and saute in a heavy pot. Remove bacon to a paper towel and drain. Pour off most of the fat. Season the chicken with salt and pepper and brown chicken on all sides in the pot. Remove and keep warm. Drain off most of the fat.

Laying Hen

Coq au Beaujolais (cont.)

Chapter 4

Poultry & Fowl

Add the drained marinated vegetables to the pot; cook over medium heat for 3 minutes. Return the chicken to the pot and stir in the flour. Add the reserved marinade and bring to a boil, scraping the bottom of the pan to loosen any brown bits. Reduce heat and simmer for 30 to 40 minutes. Taste for salt and pepper.

Peel the pearl onions and cook them in salted water until just tender. Refresh under cold water; drain. Wash and slice the mushrooms and blanch them in a pot of water for 2 minutes; drain.

To finish the dish, add a bit more wine to thin and refresh the sauce. Simmer until hot. Transfer the chicken to a platter and arrange the bacon, mushrooms and onions on top. Skim off any fat from the sauce and strain over the chicken. Sprinkle with fresh parsley and serve immediately. Makes 4 to 6 servings.

Laying Hen

CHAPTER 5

Magnificent Meats

Steer

Young Grunter

Lamb

Deer

DINNER WITH FILLMORE

**Magnificent
Meats**

The term of office of Millard Fillmore from 1850 to 1853 was uninspired as far as politics were concerned. In fact, some historians label his term a "regime of conveniences."

Fillmore was the first of our presidents to have a real bathtub with centrally heated running water. His wife Abigail installed the first library in the White House. The expense and notion of having a room designed exclusively for the display and reading of books shocked the citizens.

More disturbing to the people of the era, however, was the innovation of an iron cookstove in the president's house. His own chef was horrified at the idea of cooking on such a "thing." The president himself had to master the stove. He was forced to pay a visit to the patent office to learn how to manipulate the stove's drafts and pulleys. Once this hurdle was overcome, the stove became standard equipment in the White House kitchen. After the newness wore off, it became a habit. The staff wondered how they had ever managed without it.

The Fillmore dinners were frequent. Thursdays were for large dinner parties in the State Dining Room. Friday evenings, the Congress was invited to a "drawing room" party. And Saturdays, in the private dining room, Abigail presided over smaller dinners. Washington Irving, Franklin Pierce and William Thackeray were often among the guests who enjoyed this steak dinner.

SHAKER FLANK STEAK

2 pounds flank steak

1 tablespoon flour

1 1/2 tablespoons butter

3/4 teaspoon salt

1/4 teaspoon pepper

2 large potatoes, peeled and cubed

2 small onions, chopped

1 carrot, chopped

1 stalk celery, chopped

Juice of 1/2 lemon

1/3 cup ketchup

Score both sides of the steak diagonally; dust with flour. Melt butter in a large skillet and brown steak on both sides. Season with salt and pepper. Add the potatoes in large cubes. Add onions, carrot and celery. Pour the lemon juice and ketchup over all. Cover and simmer for an hour or longer, until tender. Serve with vegetable sauce over the steak. Serves 4.

Steer

White House Corned Beef Hash

Chapter 5

Magnificent Meats

Through the years a common favorite served to guests at the White House was Corned Beef Hash.

A prominent businessman wrote that the first time he was invited for a meal at the White House was as a guest of President McKinley. He was served Corned Beef Hash. It was not his favorite dish, but, since he was a guest, he ate it.

A few years later, he lunched with President Theodore Roosevelt and again sat down to Corned Beef Hash. Then during the Taft administration he was invited to breakfast. Taft, who had a robust appetite, munched on his large steak, but offered his guest something different. You guessed it—Corned Beef Hash. The man began to think this was some type of joke. His last visit to the White House was during Herbert Hoover's administration. The meal, of course, was hash.

Hash is usually served plain, but at the White House it was served with a poached egg. Here is one version of the recipe.

Corned Beef Hash

4 medium boiled potatoes

1/2 cup hot milk

2 tablespoons butter

2 cups corned beef, minced

2 tablespoons minced onion

2 tablespoons finely chopped celery

2 tablespoons chopped green pepper

Salt and pepper to taste

Mash potatoes with a fork; beat in hot milk and butter. Add minced corned beef, onion, celery and green pepper. Season with salt and pepper. Form into patties and bake on a grill or spread into a greased pan and bake for 30 minutes, until golden brown. If made in a pan, cut into squares when ready to serve. Top with a poached egg and serve hot. Makes 6 servings.

If you have one, an electric poacher may be used to poach eggs. If poaching by hand, use a saucepan or skillet. Add 2 cups water or enough to make 1 1/2 inches in depth to the pan. Season water with salt and add 1 tablespoon vinegar. Bring water to a boil. Break the egg into a cup. Hold the cup in one hand and swirl the boiling water with a spoon in the other hand to form a whirlpool in the center of the pan. Slip the egg into the center of the whirlpool and reduce heat to simmer. As the egg spins, the white will wrap around the yolk and form an oval shape. Cook to desired doneness. Remove with a slotted spoon and trim any ragged edges with scissors. Drain well; serve on top of hash.

Cow

A Jackson Festive Feast

Chapter 5

Magnificent Meats

When Andrew Jackson was living at his Tennessee home, The Hermitage, his neighbors referred to him as "the prince of hospitality." He and Mrs. Jackson, Rachel, entertained many people. The streetsweeper and the peddler were as welcome as the president, statesman and general. The Jacksons were renowned for their hospitality in a country where hospitality was a common virtue.

After the general's election, Rachel faced a life in Washington with misgiving, yet was prepared for the move. She did not, however, live to get to Washington to become first lady. The president solved the problem by appointing his two nieces to share the social honors of the White House.

In 1836, Jackson put on an unforgettable Christmas party. Six children were living in the White House: President Jackson's private secretary had four and his adopted son had two. Children from all over Washington received this invitation: "The children of President Jackson's family request you to join them on Christmas Day, at four o'clock p.m., in a frolic in the East Room."

At the appointed time, a band stationed in the corridor struck up the "President's March." The children were formed into lines, the younger ones leading, and marshaled into supper. The rooms were decorated with garlands, flowers and greens. The fireplaces were burning brightly with yule logs. And the president's famous chef, Vivart, had created his awesome ices and confections. One of these frozen marvels was iced fruits—oranges, apples, peaches, grapes gathered at one end of the table. The other end had iced vegetables—corn, carrots, beans and squashes. There were candies, cakes, confections of every conceivable design. Each guest was given one of these tempting repasts as a souvenir to take home.

The main course was a favorite of the president: Roast Loin of Pork with Apricots.

Roast Loin of Pork with Apricots

3 pounds boned loin of pork

1 cup plum-dried apricots

4 tablespoons sugar

2 cups water

Black pepper and salt

1/4 teaspoon dry thyme

2 tablespoons soft butter

Remove roast from refrigerator at least 2 hours before roasting. Trim off any extra fat, leaving a thin layer. Meanwhile, put the apricots in a saucepan with the sugar and water. Bring to a boil; simmer covered for 10 minutes. The apricots should be firm but soft; drain well. Make horizontal cuts in the pork at 1-inch intervals, to a depth of 1 1/2 inches.

Young Grunter

A Jackson Festive Feast (cont.)

Chapter 5

Magnificent Meats

Season entire roast with freshly ground pepper. Sprinkle only the fat with salt. Push the apricots into the slits, pressing them in as deep as possible inasmuch as the meat will contract during cooking and push the apricots to the surface. Tie roast at intervals with string and place in a foil-lined baking pan. Sprinkle the thyme over the meat and spread soft butter over the surface. Bake at 400 degrees for 1 1/4 to 1 1/2 hours.

Baste with juices from time to time. About halfway through the cooking time, add a bit of water or juice; cover with foil and continue to bake. This prevents the apricots from caramelizing. When ready to serve, remove the strings and transfer to a heated platter. Pour off any excess fat from the pan and glaze the roast with the juices. Let it rest for a few minutes. Slice and serve, garnished with broiled peach halves stuffed with chutney. Serves 6 to 8.

Young Grunter

The French Pot Roast

5
CHAPTER

Magnificent Meats

During the cold, lean months of winter, think of a food that is just right to fortify you against the rigors of the season. Chances are, nothing sounds better than a steaming pot of hearty beef stew. The oven warms your kitchen and makes you feel nurtured.

A favorite winter meat is beef. This dish does not require an expensive sirloin or tenderloin but is best when a choice cut is used.

The best way to prepare it is by a moist, low-heat cooking called braising. In Italy, they have their osso bucca. In America, we have Yankee pot roast and in France they have Boeuf a la Mode.

Boeuf a la Mode is the most common winter dish in France. It had its beginnings during the 19th century in Paris where the meat merchant would parade his finest steer, garlanded with flowers, through streets lined with cheering crowds. This parade gave rise to a restaurant called Boeuf a la Mode, whose sign showed a steer decked out in the latest fashion. The recipe has been around for years, but the new name revived it for all to enjoy. This recipe dates from 1659.

Boeuf a la Mode (pot roast)

1 4-pound chuck roast
Salt and black pepper
3 tablespoons bacon fat
3 tablespoons oil
1 onion,1 carrot,1 celery stick chopped
1 clove garlic, minced
3 slices cooked bacon
3 cups dry red wine
1 bouquet garni

Season the beef with salt and pepper. Heat half of the bacon fat and oil in a pot just large enough to hold the beef and vegetables. Brown the beef on all sides and transfer to a platter. Discard the fat.

Heat the remaining bacon fat and oil and add chopped onion, carrot, celery and garlic. Cook over medium heat for a few minutes or until soft. Return beef to pot and drape bacon over it. Add wine and bouquet garni. Bring to a gentle boil. Press a tent of parchment or foil over the beef and cover with a lid. Bake at 325 degrees for 1 hour. Prepare Vegetable Garnish.

Vegetable Garnish

3 carrots
3 new potatoes
2 turnips
3 small leeks, green part removed
3 tablespoons chopped parsley

While the beef cooks, peel carrots, potatoes and turnips. Cut into 2-inch cubes or carve them into fancy shapes. Cut leeks in half lengthwise and wash well. Add the vegetables to beef and cook for another 1 1/2 hours.

To serve, remove beef and slice. Place on a warm platter and surround with the vegetables. Keep warm. Remove bouquet garni from the pot and skim off the fat. Puree sauce and taste for seasoning. If it needs thickening, add 1 tablespoon cornstarch dissolved in 1 tablespoon Madeira. Let it thicken and pour over meat. Garnish with parsley. Serves 6.

Carrot

FOR ST. PATRICK

CHAPTER 5

Magnificent Meats

When St. Patrick lay on his death bed, he asked his followers to celebrate, not lament his passing—the pious origin, perhaps, of the custom of drinking whiskey at wakes. (Our word whiskey comes from the Gaelic usque-beathe, literally "water of life.") St. Patrick would probably not have approved of the green beer served in modern taverns, but he wouldn't have objected to a pint or two of Guinness to wash down the traditional corned beef and cabbage.

A spinoff of this dish became popular in New England and in the Midwest at the turn of the century and remains a favorite today. We know it as Red Flannel Hash, a tasty change from the regular corned beef and cabbage St. Patrick's Day.

Red Flannel Hash

2 cups corned beef

2 cups cooked beets

3 1/2 cups cooked potatoes

1 onion, chopped

Salt and pepper

1 1/2 teaspoons Worcestershire sauce

Light cream, as needed

Bacon drippings or butter

Cube corned beef, beets and potatoes; add chopped onion and season with salt and pepper. Add Worcestershire sauce and enough cream to hold together. Heat bacon drippings or butter in heavy cast iron skillet. Spread the hash evenly over the bottom. Warm over low heat, watching carefully. Loosen the edges and shake the skillet to prevent burning. When it is nice and brown and a crust forms on the bottom, turn with a spatula. Serve on a warm platter. Serves 6 to 8.

Beets

DINNER IN VIENNA

Vienna's reputation for cakes and pastries is the pride of Austrian cooking. Each day hundreds of these are served with clouds of vanilla-scented whipped cream. At the same time, there are ample recipes for soups and roasts.

Vienna's Hotel Sacher is famous for its boiled beef with beef soup. With this recipe two dishes are produced from one pot—the soup to begin the meal and the boiled beef for the main course.

In Austria fresh beef is used for boiling and only the best quality cuts are used. The Emperor Franz Joseph is supposed to have eaten this dish daily. The vegetables with which the beef is cooked are strained off and the meat is served garnished with freshly cooked vegetables. Sauteed potatoes are required. Other accompaniments might include creamed spinach, savory cabbage, braised lettuce and a horseradish or dill sauce.

BOILED BEEF DINNER

1 pound marrow bones

1 tablespoon butter

1 large onion, halved, not peeled

3 medium carrots

2 small stalks celery, sliced

1 green or red pepper, diced

1 small parsnip, sliced

1 small turnip, diced

2 leeks, halved

Bunch of parsley, chopped

3 1/2-pound cut of beef, topside or silverside

1 teaspoon marjoram

6 black peppercorns

Salt to taste

Scald marrow bones in hot water; rinse in cold water and place in heavy pan. Cover pot and place over low heat. Allow bones to lightly brown until fat on them begins to melt. If there is not enough fat on the bones, add butter and place onion, cut-side down, in pan to brown.

Add carrots, celery, pepper, parsnip, turnip, leeks and parsley; cover pan and continue to cook for 10 minutes.

Arrange beef among the vegetables and cover with 5 to 6 pints cold water. Add marjoram, peppercorns and salt. Bring liquid to just a boil over high heat then simmer, uncovered, over very low heat until meat is very tender, about 2 1/2 hours. Do not let liquid boil, or, if it does, remove any scum.

When meat is very tender, lift it out carefully. Keep hot and moisten with some of the liquid so it does not dry out. To finish the soup, first strain the liquid through a fine sieve. Allow soup to cool a bit; skim off any excess fat. The soup may then be reheated, seasoned and served.

Slice beef across the grain and serve garnished with the vegetables and with crisp sauteed potatoes. The sauce is passed separately. Serves 6 to 8. (Boiled beef with soup still appears on the Hotel Sacher menu.)

Onion

Stir Fry Sirloin

Chapter 5

Magnificent Meats

The quick stir-fried dishes of China are derived from one of the world's most ancient cuisines. They are the blending of thousands of years of careful experimentation. All are quick and easily prepared.

If you admit that you love Chinese food but are afraid to cook it because it is too different and exotic, change your mind. Admittedly, Chinese food is different but the stir-fry method always produces great results.

The execution of stir-fry cooking is easy. Apart from a good-sized chopping board, a sharp knife to cut the vegetables, fish or meat, all that is needed is a large, heavy-bottomed frying pan—or, even better, a Chinese wok. The wok is a wide, curved-bottomed pan which is traditionally used in China for stir-frying. The advantage of cooking with a wok is that the heat is concentrated in the center of the base of the pan and food can be jostled toward or away from the heat as you choose.

All the ingredients should be prepared before you start cooking, for you will not have time, once you have started, to chop or cut any ingredients. Thinly sliced meat is cooked through almost as quickly as it touches the pan. Even pork is cooked in a matter of minutes. Pork is the most popular meat used in stir-frying, with beef and chicken close behind. But shrimp, chicken and duck are used if your mood calls for them.

Fillet or sirloin roast should be cut into 2-inch pieces and sliced 1/8 inch thick. Marinate strips for at least a half hour in a mixture of cornstarch blended with water, soy sauce and rice wine or sherry. The vegetables are cooked for minutes only. Beforehand, blanch them in boiling water and drain and dry. They should be cooked in a little hot oil, moistened with a bit of stock and accented with soy or oyster sauce and a little sake, dry white wine or sherry, to make a thing of beauty out of a humdrum accompaniment to meat.

Sirloin Strips with Oriental Dressing

1 1/2 to 2 pounds sirloin steak

2 tablespoons peanut oil

2 tablespoons shallots, chopped

1 tablespoon soy sauce

1/2 cup beef stock

2 tablespoons oyster sauce

1 pound assorted vegetables of contrasting color and texture

1/4 teaspoon ground pepper

Squeeze of lemon juice

Pinch of sugar

Pinch of cayenne

Chopped green onion for garnish

Steer

Stir Fry Sirloin (cont.)

5
Chapter

Magnificent Meats

Cut meat into thin strips about 2 or 3 inches long. Heat wok over high heat; add oil. When oil is hot, drop in the strips of meat, a few at a time. Cook over high heat until brown on the outside but rare inside. Remove as they cook; set aside.

Lower heat and add more oil, if needed. Cook shallots until just tender. Stir in soy sauce and stock. Let reduce a bit and add oyster sauce. Add the vegetables and cook for a couple of minutes. Season with pepper, lemon juice, sugar and cayenne. Return meat to the pan and reheat for about 10 seconds or until hot. Transfer to a warm dish; sprinkle with chopped green onions and serve. Makes 8 servings.

Steer

A Winter Supper

Chapter

5

*Magnificent
Meats*

In the winter cold and darkness, a light from a kitchen window is a true beacon that promises warmth and delightful smells. A truly great winter scent is that of a bubbling pot of beans.

More and more people are discovering that dried beans are economical, delicious and versatile, besides being highly nutritious. They provide significant quantities of protein and iron. Beans contain little fat and are a great source of fiber and bulk along with several B-complex vitamins.

Try this recipe using dried beans to trim calories, cut food costs and provide a tasty and nourishing meal.

Beef and Bean Supper

1 pound dried pinto beans

1 medium onion, chopped

1 clove garlic, minced

2 tablespoons olive oil

1 pound cubed or ground beef

3 cups canned tomatoes

1 can (8 ounces) tomato sauce

1 teaspoon salt

1/4 teaspoon pepper

2 bay leaves

Wash and sort beans; place in large, heavy kettle. Cover with at least 2 inches of water; let soak overnight. Drain beans and cover with water. Bring to a boil. Reduce heat, cover and let simmer for 1 hour.

Saute onions and garlic in oil until tender. Add beef and brown, stirring often. Drain off any pan drippings; add to the beans. Add tomatoes, tomato sauce, salt, pepper and bay leaves. Cover and simmer at least two hours, stirring occasionally. Makes 8 to 10 servings. (Any type of dried bean may be substituted for pinto beans.)

Porridge

A Summer Brisket

5
CHAPTER

Magnificent Meats

Slow cooking in the oven at its lowest setting is a sure way to avoid the heat of a summer kitchen. This cooking may be done while you are away or at night while you sleep. Slow cooking gives you the freedom to enjoy your summer days.

Slow cooking is one of the oldest and simplest ways of food preparation, requiring no special rules or equipment. It is essential that you experiment with your temperature control until you find the ideal low setting. Cheaper cuts of meat are best slow cooked in a liquid, in a pan or casserole with a tight-fitting lid to prevent the food from drying out. If you are roasting a cut of meat, it should be wrapped in foil.

A summer cooking recipe that I find easy is a brisket of beef, served hot or cold. A brisket of beef gently simmered in wine with vegetables makes an ideal summer meal. It may be cooked slowly during the day or at night, then warmed or served cold.

Summer Brisket of Beef

1 large onion, sliced

1 red or green pepper, sliced

2 teaspoons chopped fresh basil

Salt and pepper

1 brisket of beef, rolled (about 4 pounds)

2 tablespoons olive oil

2 cloves garlic, crushed

6 medium tomatoes, skinned and sliced

1 1/2 cups dry white wine

1 tablespoon flour

1/2 cup pitted black olives

2 tablespoons chopped parsley

In a flame proof casserole dish, put onion, pepper and half the basil; sprinkle with salt and pepper. Put the tied brisket on top and brush with oil. Sprinkle on the garlic, the rest of the basil and salt and pepper. Top with tomatoes; pour in wine. Bring to a boil on the stove. Cover tightly, and cook in a 180-degree oven for 8 hours or overnight.

When ready to serve, remove meat and put casserole on stove. Bring liquid to a boil and reduce liquid by half. Mix butter and flour into a paste (*beurre manie*) and whisk in a little at a time. Stir until sauce thickens; add olives. Remove string from meat; pour some of sauce over meat. Sprinkle with parsley and serve. Extra sauce may be spooned from a sauce boat, or you can forget the sauce and just serve brisket cold, with any dressing and a salad for a cool summer meal.

Cow

THE BEST VEAL

5

CHAPTER

Magnificent Meats

Veal—the meat of young calves that have been specially reared for tenderness—is delicate and requires careful cooking. Until fairly recently, veal was not too plentiful in the butcher shops. One reason for this is that it does not keep well and must be used within three or four days of purchase.

Today, the demand for veal is increasing, partly as a result of foreign travel and an appreciation of French and Italian fare in restaurants.

The best veal is recognized by the fine grain, firm and smooth texture of the meat, and the white and satiny fat. The meat should be almost white or just faintly tinted pink. When cooking veal, be aware that it has very little fat and is inclined to be dry. To avoid this the cooking temperature should be kept low and the roast supplemented by additional fat. This is done by spreading it with butter or covering with a thin strip of pork fat. The tendency toward dryness may be counteracted by wrapping the roast in foil to increase the steam in the package. Try this roast veal, wrapped in foil, and seasoned with fresh herbs.

ROAST VEAL IN FOIL

3-pound loin of veal, boned, rolled
    and tied
4 tablespoons softened butter
Freshly ground black pepper
2 to 3 sprigs fresh rosemary

Spread roast with butter; sprinkle with freshly ground black pepper. Sprinkle rosemary over roast and let it stand to come to room temperature. Preheat oven to 400 degrees.

Loosely cover roast with foil. Be careful to leave enough space inside the foil for air to circulate. Place in a roasting pan on small rack and roast at 400 degrees for 15 to 20 minutes to seal in juices. Reduce temperature to 325 degrees for the remaining cooking time,

depending on weight. Allow 55 minutes per pound for roasting. Thirty minutes before it is done, carefully open foil and let roast brown. Remove meat to warm platter; remove string and keep warm. Pour juices from foil into roasting pan and make sauce by adding 1/3 cup stock and 1/3 cup dry white wine to juices in pan; bring to a boil. Mix 1 tablespoon butter and 1 tablespoon flour into a paste and gradually crumble into the sauce. Continue stirring and reduce sauce by half. Season with salt, pepper and a little lemon juice. Strain sauce into a sauce boat and serve with roast. Serves 6.

Calf

Twelfth-Night

On the evening of January 6th we celebrate Twelfth-Night of the feast of Epiphany, hailing the conclusion of the medieval Christmas festivities. In many regions of the world, this is an occasion for a grand feast. In searching for such a dish, I came upon a veal recipe called Twelfth-Night Roast Veal. The length of the recipe might indicate that it would take 12 days to prepare. Not so. In spite of the large number of ingredients, it may be made ahead of time and reheated.

Twelfth-Night Roast Veal

11 tablespoons butter, divided

1 boned 3-pound veal roast, tied

1 medium carrot, chopped

1 medium onion, chopped

2 sprigs parsley

1 bay leaf

1/3 cup white wine

2 tablespoons shallots, minced

1/2 pound mushrooms, sliced

Salt and white pepper to taste

1/4 cup white wine

3 tablespoons flour

2 cups milk, scalded

1/8 teaspoon nutmeg

2 egg yolks

1/2 cup grated Gruyere cheese

8 thin slices ham

8 thin slices Gruyere

1 tablespoon grated Gruyere

Melt 4 tablespoons of the butter in a roasting pan large enough to hold roast. Place roast in pan. Bake at 375 degrees for 15 minutes, turning the veal on all sides.

Remove veal from pan and make a bed of carrots, onions, parsley and bay leaf. Place veal on top. Bake for another 15 minutes. Add 1/3 cup wine and bake another 20 minutes or until juices are clear. Remove from oven and let veal rest a few minutes.

Prepare a druxelles (mushroom mixture) by melting 3 tablespoons butter in skillet. Add shallots and cook a couple of minutes. Add mushrooms and salt and pepper to taste. Cook until moisture evaporates. Add 1/4 cup wine; cook until liquid is completely evaporated.

In saucepan, melt 3 tablespoons butter. Add flour and stir in the milk until blended. Remove from heat and add salt, white pepper and nutmeg to taste. Cook, stirring constantly, until thickened. Remove from heat and beat in the slightly whipped yolks. Stir in 1/2 cup grated cheese; stir until melted.

Slice veal into 8 slices. Place slices on an oven-proof platter. On each piece, place a bit of druxelles, 1 slice of ham and 1 slice of cheese. Cover with sauce and sprinkle with remaining grated cheese.

This dish may be prepared up to this point ahead of time. When ready to serve, bake at 375 degrees for 30 minutes. If desired place under a broiler for color the last few minutes. Serves 8.

Butter Churn

An Italian Delicacy

5

Chapter

Magnificent Meats

The region of Lazio, which surrounds Rome, was at one time mostly marshland. In modern times it has been drained and is now cultivated to provide many of the fresh foods for Rome.

One of the first cookbooks ever printed was compiled by the Vatican library. It appeared in 1474 and was based on the culinary writings of Marcus Apicus, a learned gourmet. Apicus spent so much money on food that eventually he could no longer live in the style to which he was accustomed, and committed suicide.

His recipes, however, lived on, and influenced both Italian and French cooking. They were adopted by the great Roman households of the Renaissance—the Borgias, Borghese, Barberinis and Farnese—who impressed many foreign leaders with their lavish banquets.

The famous dishes of Lazio and Rome are still served for special occasions. Roast suckling pig, baby lamb and goat, all stuffed with herbs and cooked on a spit, along with numerous veal dishes, are common. Since there is not enough land to provide grazing for large herds, these animals are sold when very young. Saltimbocca is one of these old and favorite veal dishes.

Saltimbocca (veal and ham rolls)

1 pound veal, cut into 8 escalopes

8 thin slices ham, raw or cooked

8 sage leaves, fresh

Salt and pepper

2 tablespoons butter

1 cup white wine

Beat veal with a rolling pin until thin and of uniform thickness. Trim ham slices so they are the same size as the veal. Cover each slice of veal with a slice of ham and a sage leaf. Roll up and secure with a toothpick so that the

toothpick lies along the side of the roll. Season with salt and pepper.

Gently saute veal rolls in butter until they are brown all over. Add wine and simmer a couple of minutes. Cover and cook over low heat for 15 minutes or until tender. Serve with fresh peas and rice. Serves 4.

Hog

BARBECUED PORK CHOPS

In New England, the first sign of spring is in mid-February with the flowing of sap in the sugar maples. From this sap comes the American delicacy, maple syrup.

The process of maple sugaring remains about the same as in early Colonial times. The rising temperatures in mid- or late-February cause the sap in the trees to expand, starting what is called the "sugar run." The Indians would just gash the bark to release the sap. Today, a hollow spike is hammered into the trunk.

A four-gallon bucket is hung on the spike to catch the sap. During a good run, the bucket has to be emptied every 25 hours. The best weather for sugaring is when a series of freezing storms is followed by a warming spell.

In the Southern United States, most barbeque sauces use honey or brown sugar to sweeten the sauce. This recipe, from Raichlen's guide to Boston dining, substitutes maple syrup to sweeten the sauce.

Pork Chops with Maple Barbecue Sauce

Sauce

4 strips bacon

1 small onion, chopped

1 mild, canned jalapeno chile pepper

1 tablespoon butter

1/2 cup maple syrup

3 tablespoons Dijon grainy mustard

2 to 3 tablespoons cider or raspberry
   vinegar

Salt and black pepper

Cut bacon into bits. Chop onions; seed and chop pepper. Melt butter in a saucepan. Add to butter the onion and pepper and cook over medium heat until onion is soft. Pour off any fat and whisk in the syrup, mustard, vinegar, salt and pepper. Simmer for a few minutes. It should be a bit sweet, sour and spicy.

Pork Chops

4 pork chops

Salt and black pepper

2 tablespoons oil

2 tablespoons butter

Heat oven to 400 degrees. Trim extra fat from chops and season with salt and pepper. In large oven-proof skillet, heat oil and butter. Add chops and brown on both sides. Pour off any fat. Pour sauce over the chops and bake at 400 degrees for 15 minutes. Serves 4.

Gridiron

Plum Good!

5

Chapter

Magnificent Meats

In late summer and fall, the early American colonist went "a-plumming" to garner fruits for winter. These fruits were preserved by bottling, jellying or drying.

In 1645, William Wood wrote describing the orchards as "within this Indian orchard are grown the ruddie cherrie and jettie plumme." These colonists discovered many kinds and colors of wild and cultivated plums, including the uniquely American beach plum. This fruit was so valued by the Long Island Indians that when they sold their lands to the colonists they reserved "all liberty and privileges of plumming."

Today, we have hundreds of varieties of plums—in colors red, purple, blue, black, gold and green, with a profusion of plum names such as samson, Santa Clara, Italian prune, angelino, royal and greengage. Some have extremely tart skins, while others, such as the greengage, possess a juicy sweetness all the way through.

The Chinese have known for centuries the pleasures of combining the tart sweetness of plum puree with pork, duck or chicken. If you have an excess of overripe plums, you can make your own Chinese plum sauce by simmering pureed plums with chili peppers, ginger root and the Chinese five-spice powder (cinnamon, fennel, star anise, cloves and hot pepper).

This plum sauce is excellent with pork, lamb and chicken. It is ideal for barbecued spareribs.

Plum-Barbecued Ribs

4 pounds lean spareribs

1 cup red plum puree

1-inch piece fresh ginger, sliced

3 or 4 green onions, chopped

1 clove garlic, minced

Dash of Tabasco sauce

3 tablespoons sherry

1 tablespoon soy sauce

1 tablespoon tomato puree

1/2 cup tomato juice

1/4 teaspoon ground cinnamon

1/4 teaspoon ground cloves

1/2 cup honey

Trim meat from the racks. Grill whole racks or cut into serving portions. In a bowl, mix plum puree, ginger, onion, garlic, Tabasco, sherry, soy sauce, tomato puree, tomato juice, cinnamon, and cloves. Marinate the ribs in the mixture 6 to 8 hours in the refrigerator. Just before grilling or roasting, dribble the honey over the ribs. Grill the ribs about 5 inches from the heat. For oven roasting, roast the ribs for 50 minutes, fat-side up at 350 degrees. Halfway through roasting time, baste with the marinade. Turn the heat up to 450 degrees for the last 10 minutes. Serves 4.

Plumb

Easter Traditions

5 CHAPTER

Magnificent Meats

Easter is a holiday rich in tradition, and a number of food customs have emerged through the years. When you plan to serve your Easter ham, you should be aware of some of the ham and Easter traditions and trivia.

Ham became a traditional Easter favorite because in pre-refrigeration days, hogs were slaughtered in the fall and cured for six or seven months—just in time for Easter dinner. One of the first forms of trade in America was in cured hams.

The custom of Easter egg decorating came from the Dutch, the same people who brought us Santa Claus. The Easter Bunny came from the Pennsylvanian Dutch. The Anglo-Saxon goddess Ostera, for whom Easter was named, was the goddess of springtime. The myth that the left hind leg of a hog was more tender than the right is because the hogs use their right leg to scratch themselves, enabling it to get more exercise.

Now that you are aware of some of the trivia connected with ham at Easter, you should try this recipe.

Ham with Peach Chutney

1 4-pound fully-cooked boneless ham

1 cup orange juice

1/4 cup brown sugar

1 can (16 ounces) peach slices in juice, drained

3/4 cup cider vinegar

1/2 small onion, minced

1/2 cup brown sugar, packed

1 apple, peeled and sliced

1 teaspoon pickling spices

Juice of 1/2 lemon

Place ham in shallow pan. Combine orange juice and brown sugar. Roast ham at 325 degrees for 1 1/2 to 2 1/4 hours, or to an internal temperature of 140 degrees when tested with a thermometer. Baste several times with the orange juice mixture while cooking. Remove from the oven; cool a few minutes. Slice and serve with Peach Chutney.

To make Peach Chutney, chop peaches coarsely. In a large saucepan, combine peaches, vinegar, onion, brown sugar, apple, pickling spices and lemon juice; simmer 20 minutes or until thickened. Let cool to room temperature if served with hot ham, or chill for cold ham. Makes 6 to 8 servings.

Peach

All About Lamb

5

CHAPTER

Magnificent Meats

About 12,000 years ago, a man in the Middle East rounded up some wild sheep as a flock to keep under supervision. He selected an animal that would provide meat for eating and also wool for clothing, and milk for drinking and making cheese.

During the Middle Ages, sheep were bred more for their wool than their meat. Many of the great churches erected at that time were built from the profits of the wool trade.

During the 19th century, a growing urban population created a greater demand for meat. Thus a breeding program was begun to produce leaner meat that could be harvested at an earlier age. In 1882 a ship called the Dunedin sailed from New Zealand with refrigeration equipment and a cargo of lambs. This was the beginning of the lamb trade from down under that continues today.

When selecting lamb, look for pink, firm and fine-grained flesh with dry white fat. As the lamb ages, the flesh color deepens and the meat acquires a more mature flavor. After a lamb passes its first birthday, it is classified as mutton.

Certain fruits and spices complement lamb and enhance its flavor. The most popular jam used throughout the world is red currant. Most Americans prefer mint jelly, and the English enjoy mint sauce with their lamb.

This recipe for lamb cutlets is made from a rack of lamb that has had the bones cut away.

Lamb Cutlets Cumberland

8 lamb cutlets
Freshly ground black pepper
1 tablespoon oil
2 tablespoons butter
Salt

Pat the cutlets dry and season with pepper. Heat the oil and butter in a large skillet and brown cutlets on both sides. Reduce heat and continue to cook for about 10 minutes, turning on time. Season with salt and arrange, overlapping in a circle, on a heated platter.

Sauce

1/2 cup lamb or beef stock
4 tablespoons red currant jelly
2 tablespoons lemon juice
1 tablespoon Worcestershire sauce
1 tablespoon cornstarch

Pour off most of the fat from the pan and add the stock, jelly, lemon juice and Worcestershire sauce. Stir over low heat until blended. Mix the cornstarch with 2 tablespoons water and stir into the pan. Boil for a minute and pour over cutlets. Garnish with fresh peas, baby carrots and watercress sprigs. Serves 4.

Ewe

THYME FOR LAMB

Chapter 5

Magnificent Meats

When Spring arrives, most gardeners and cooks begin to poke around in the garden in the hope that some of their herbs have survived the winter. The one herb that seems to best handle the cold of winter is thyme, known as the "poor man's herb" because it is so easy to grow. It rates high in popularity with everyone.

Used to flavor stews, soups and sauces, thyme goes well with dishes in which wine is used. There are many varieties of this herb, both wild and cultivated.

Lemon thyme adds zest to scrambled eggs, egg sandwich spreads and creamed eggs. When roasting beef, lamb or veal, mix some thyme with salt and black pepper and rub over the meat before cooking. Add a bit of thyme to any casserole of meat or chicken shortly before the cooking time is up. When added to melted butter, it adds to the flavor of lobster and shrimp and makes an excellent dressing for carrots, mushrooms, onions and new potatoes.

For a real treat this spring take a little thyme to try this roast lamb shoulder.

ROAST LAMB SHOULDER

3-pound shoulder of lamb, boned
2 tablespoons olive oil
Salt and fresh ground pepper
6 sprigs thyme
6 sprigs rosemary
6 sprigs bay leaves

Ask your butcher to bone and trim a shoulder of lamb ready for rolling, but do not let him roll it. Lay the lamb out flat; brush with olive oil and sprinkle with salt and pepper. Place 2 sprigs each of thyme, rosemary and bay leaves on the lamb; roll up and tie securely.

Place 4 more sprigs of each of the herbs around the lamb. Brush the meat with olive oil and roast in a preheated 325-degree oven for 1 1/2 hours for pink meat or cook for another 15 minutes for well done. Thirty minutes before the end of cooking time, increase the temperature to 400 degrees to brown well. Transfer to a warm platter and let rest a few minutes before carving.

Ram

THE DEER STORY

5

CHAPTER

Magnificent Meats

Man has been eating deer since prehistoric times, and there have been periods when it was the principal human food. Prehistoric man hunted the stag in China and Borneo 500,000 years ago. It is revealed that 110,000 years ago deer was the third most important food, and by 23,000 years ago it had become number one. White-tailed deer was eaten by prehistoric American Indians in what is now New England, and red deer was long a favorite in what is now the Soviet Union. Deer was common in early Palestine and Mesopotamia in the 7th Century B.C. And the ancient Hebrews ate deer with the permission of Deuteronomy 14:4-5.

In the pre-Roman period, the Gauls rode after hounds in pursuit of deer, offering a sacrificial ceremony following the hunt.

In 1455, the count of Anjou served a quarter of a deer as the first course of a ceremonial feast.

When venison lovers reached America, they described it as "the home of the deer," which is not correct, since this animal's origin was in Eurasia. By the time of the Revolution Massachusetts had imposed restrictions on deer hunting in all the colonies except Georgia.

I have no idea which species make the best eating. The order is in dispute, but the European roebuck has headed the list since medieval times. Second would be the fallow deer of Europe. Next come the three American species: the white-tailed, the black-tailed, and finally the mule deer.

Game used to be the province of hunters, but today it is available at butcher shops and specialty markets. Domestic deer is now raised like cattle; wild venison cannot be sold. To enjoy it, you must be a hunter yourself or have a hunter friend. Game lacks the benefit of a regular food supply and a vitamin-enriched diet. The meat is leaner than that of domestic animals. Venison contains only two percent fat. Because of this, it is usually bolstered by the addition of fat to prevent it from being unpalatably dry. If you are fond of venison or elk and have a supply available, then here is a recipe to try.

BLACKENED VENISON WITH CITRUS SOUR CREAM

1 1/2 pounds venison loin

2 tablespoons whole white peppercorns

1 tablespoon salt

Sauce

Cut venison into medallions (small 1/2-inch steaks). Coarsely grind the peppercorns and salt in a mortar and pestle.

Prepare the sauce.

Deer

The Deer Story (cont.)

5
CHAPTER

Magnificent Meats

Sauce

Juice of 3 oranges

Juice of 1 or 2 lemons

A pinch of cayenne pepper

3/4 cup dairy sour cream

Salt and white pepper

Combine the orange and lemon juice with the cayenne in a saucepan. Boil over high heat until reduced to 3 tablespoons. Remove from heat; stir in sour cream and season with salt and white pepper.

Just before serving, heat a heavy skillet over high heat for 3 minutes. Dust meat with the pepper mixture. Add the butter to the skillet and heat until smoking; add medallions. Cook for 1 minute on each side. The meat should be charred on the outside and rare in the middle. Place on a warm platter and spoon sauce on top. Garnish with a few sprigs of cilantro and serve. Makes 4 servings.

Deer

The Secret of Venison

5

Chapter

Magnificent Meats

When the autumn air is crisp and the leaves are turning to wonderful colors, you will find clusters of men and women dressed in brightly colored hats and jackets. As they pile into pickup trucks and campers, you know that they are about to celebrate an age-old ritual. It's hunting season again.

I have never been much of a hunter, but each year I receive lots of requests for a good way to cook venison. I seldom have cooked wild game of any kind, but I have collected a number of recipes for their preparation. When I checked my files I found two recipes marked with a star and a note, indicating that good old Joe fixed this last year and reported it was excellent.

One of my hunter friends claims he can prepare venison that actually tastes like tenderloin. His secret lies in removing the fascia or white membranes separating the muscles. If you do not remove this membrane, it will be tough and chewy.

Venison is by nature a dry meat and should not be overcooked. Steaks or kabobs are improved by marinating.

Venison Kabobs

2 large green peppers, quartered

1 pound fresh mushroom caps

1 stick (1/2 cup) butter

2 pounds venison, cut into cubes

2 or 3 tomatoes, cubed

2 or 3 medium onions, quartered

Garlic salt to taste

Pepper to taste

Briefly saute green peppers and mushrooms in butter until tender-crisp. Drain; reserve butter. Alternate meat and vegetables on skewers. Grill kabobs about 6 inches over medium-hot coals 10 to 12 minutes, basting with reserved butter. Use garlic salt and pepper to taste. Makes about 8 kabobs.

Grilled Venison Steaks

10 to 12 pounds venison, from hind quarter

1 bottle (16 ounces) Italian dressing

1 package (2.75 ounces) dry onion soup mix

3/4 cup butter, melted

2 teaspoons pepper

Slice muscle cross grain into 1-inch-thick steaks. Remove any white membrane surrounding steaks. Combine Italian dressing and soup mix; stir. Place steaks in shallow dish; cover with marinade. I find that a large zip-lock bag works well to turn the steaks easily and quickly. Marinate steaks in refrigerator for

Hart

THE SECRET OF VENISON (CONT.)

Chapter 5

Magnificent Meats

1 to 4 hours, or overnight. Turn steaks every now and then.

Combine butter with pepper; mix well. Set aside. Remove steaks from marinade and grill about 5 inches from hot coals for 8 to 10 minutes per side. Baste while grilling with butter mixture. Serves 10 to 12 hungry hunters.

Hart

A Swedish Joke

Chapter 5

Magnificent Meats

On a trip to Sweden, I kept asking when we were going to sample some of the famous Swedish Meatballs. Days went by until one day at noon we stopped at a local restaurant which advertised a special of the day: Swedish Meatballs. When they arrived, they were served in a tasty sauce along with boiled potatoes and lingonberry jam.

Now to the funny part of the meatball story: I could detect a seasoning in the meatballs, but was not sure what it was. I had noticed that the chef had his membership certificate for the Chaine des Rotisseurs displayed in the hall, so, also being a member, I went over to the kitchen. He was very cordial and invited me into the kitchen.

I asked about the seasoning in the meatballs, he did not seem to understand my question. I then asked him to show me the spices he used in the recipe. He showed me those that he used and then I realized that the taste I had detected was allspice. I asked how much he used and he started to laugh. He explained that he really had to be honest, for he had not made the meatballs nor the sauce for—it was purchased frozen and had been made in America. All he had to do was heat it.

Later in the trip I did manage to get a Swedish Meatball recipe which I will share with you. If it is as good as the frozen version, and I think you will enjoy it.

Swedish Meatballs

4 1/2 tablespoons bread crumbs or cold
    mashed potatoes
1/3 cup milk
1/3 cup thick cream
14 ounces ground meat (beef or veal with
    a bit of pork)
1 1/4 teaspoons salt
1/4 teaspoon white or black pepper
2 tablespoons finely chopped
  yellow onion, sauteed or raw
1/8 teaspoon allspice, or more to taste

Mix bread crumbs or potatoes with milk and cream; let stand at least 10 minutes. Mix meat with salt, pepper, onion and allspice; add to breadcrumb mixture. Stir until smooth, but not too much or mixture will become dry. Taste for seasoning.

Form into small meatballs of uniform size. Fry in a little butter in frying pan. Shake during cooking so meatballs stay round until evenly browned. Serve with a brown sauce and lingonberry sauce, if served hot. Meatballs may be served warm or cold for any meal, but always with the lingonberry sauce. This recipe will feed 5 or 6.

6

Chapter

Gifts from the Sea

a Lobster

Crab

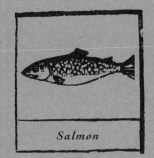

Salmon

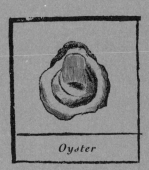

Oyster

Famous Crab Cakes

6 CHAPTER

Gifts from the Sea

There are 4,400 different species of crab, but the one thing they have in common is all true crabs are edible.

People the world over eat crabs. In the United States, crab is second in seafood popularity, even outdistancing the symbol of luxury, lobster. (Shrimp is number one.)

In June, the crab most renowned is the blue crab or softshelled crab. Providers of this American specialty are found in the Chesapeake Bay and the Gulf Coast. The Maryland crab meat comes in three forms: lump meat (large, white, meaty chunks from the body, used for crab cakes and salads); flake meat (small, white pieces from the body—used for soups and sautes); and claw meat (sweet but brownish in color—for dipping).

There was much hullabaloo engendered in the Senate in January 1963 when Sen. Jay Glen Beall, R-Maryland, inflicted a gastronomic attack on the Democratic administration. He charged that the crab cakes served at the Senate Restaurant were an insult to his state. A few days after this public declaration, he announced he had received support from a Democrat—the wife of the governor of Maryland, Avalynne Tawes—and waved Mrs. Tawes' letter that included the recipe for true Maryland Crab Cakes. It is not known if the Senate dining room changed its recipe as a result, but here is the authentic version, according to genuine crab-cake fanciers.

Maryland Crab Cakes

1 pound lump crab meat (2 1/2 cups)

2 cups fresh bread crumbs

2 eggs, well beaten

1 tablespoon Dijon mustard

White pepper and salt

1/4 cup chopped green onions

1 teaspoon Old Bay Seasoning
 (I added this seasoning)

1/2 cup mayonnaise

Corn, peanut or vegetable oil

In a mixing bowl, combine the crab meat, picked over, with 1 1/2 cups of the bread crumbs, eggs, mustard, a dash of white pepper and salt, onions, Bay Seasoning and mayonnaise. Blend well but gently, leaving the crab-meat lumps as big as possible. Shape into 10 patties of equal size. Coat with remaining bread crumbs and refrigerate.

In a large skillet, heat at least 2 tablespoons oil. When hot, cook cakes in batches, adding more oil as needed. Brown for about 2 1/2 minutes on each side. Drain on a paper towel and serve hot with a wedge of lemon and tartar sauce.

Crab

Lobster Newburg

Chapter 6

Gifts from the Sea

William Waldorf Astor, son of John Jacob Astor III, was wealthy, intelligent, ambitious and considered a snob by his friends. He ventured into politics for a time but failed in this effort.

His real estate holdings were vast and in 1890 he built the Waldorf section of The Waldorf-Astoria on the corner of Fifth Avenue and 34th Street, where his mansion had stood. He leased the property to George Boldt and Oscar Tschirky, better known as Oscar of the Waldorf. These two men would make The Waldorf-Astoria synonymous with luxury, comfort and fine dining. Before the advent of The Waldorf-Astoria, eating out in a hotel was a rarity, as wealthy people generally entertained in their mansions.

Soon after the opening in 1893, Waldorf salad was featured on the hotel's menu and became a favorite of thousands of Americans. Oscar felt that to properly present three of his dishes on the menu, he needed a special dish that could keep food piping hot.

The design had to be elegant and practical. In addition, it had to fit into the sumptuous surroundings of The Waldorf. Thus was born the chafing dish. In a short time, most every home boasted a chafing dish in order to properly serve the signature dishes of The Waldorf. Chicken a la King, Lobster Newburg and Welsh Rarebit are still served in the hotel. This Newburg recipe is for you to try.

Lobster Newburg

6 tablespoons butter

3 tablespoons flour

4 cups half and half cream

1 teaspoon salt

1/8 teaspoon white pepper

Dash of nutmeg

3 egg yolks, beaten

1/2 cup sherry

1 pound fresh mushrooms, sliced

2 cups cooked, diced lobster

In a saucepan, melt 3 tablespoons butter; blend in flour. Over low heat, gradually add the cream, stirring constantly until thickened. Add the salt, pepper and nutmeg. Beat a small amount of the sauce into the egg yolks and add the egg yolk mixture to the remaining sauce. Stir constantly until smooth and thick. Add the wine; cook for 2 minutes. In another pan, melt the rest of the butter; saute the mushrooms. Add the lobster and heat through. Combine the mushrooms and lobster to the sauce and cook for 2 or 3 minutes. Transfer to a chafing dish and serve hot over heated patty shells or rice. Serves 8.

a Lobster

The Popularity of Salmon

Many years ago, Dickens wrote, "Salmon and poverty go together." If the old boy were alive today and ventured into a fish market, he would have to change his line.

Today, this red-fleshed fish is the ocean aristocrat, costing as much per pound as prime beef. Salmon was so common in Colonial America that many indentured servants had a clause in their contracts limiting the number of times the fish could be served each week.

The migratory instinct of this fish is as keen as any bird's. They have been known to swim 2,500 miles to return to their native river for spawning. The word salmon comes from the Latin salire, "to leap or to jump."

This great fish once plied the Seine, the Thames and the Rhine, not to mention the Hudson and most Connecticut rivers. Today, the major regions that provide us with fresh salmon are the Atlantic, off the coast of Canada, the British Isles, Scandinavia and the Pacific Northwest.

There are any number of preparations for salmon. Its natural fats help keep it moist during grilling or broiling. It holds together when poached or baked and is equally good served hot or cold. If you plan to serve it chilled, let it cool in the poaching liquid before refrigerating.

When the weather warms, you should be able to grill this dish outside on your barbecue.

Grilled Salmon with Soy Sauce and Spinach Ricotta

2 1/2 to 3 pounds skinless salmon fillets
1 cup soy sauce
2 cloves garlic, minced
1/2 cup cider vinegar
Spinach Ricotta

Remove any bones from the fillets and cut into serving pieces. Combine the soy sauce, garlic and vinegar and pour this mixture over salmon fillets. Marinate the fish for 1 1/2

hours. Heat coals to white hot. Make Spinach Ricotta.

Spinach Ricotta

3/4 pound fresh spinach
1 medium onion, finely chopped
3 tablespoons butter
1 pound ricotta cheese
Salt, pepper and nutmeg
1 stick (1/2 cup) butter, melted

Stem and wash spinach. In a saucepan, blanch it for about a minute. Refresh under

Spinach

The Popularity of Salmon (cont.)

Chapter 6

*Gifts from
the Sea*

cold water and squeeze out as much water as possible. Melt the 3 tablespoons butter in a skillet and saute the onion for 3 or 4 minutes; do not brown. Let cool. Puree the spinach, onions and ricotta. Season to taste with salt, pepper and nutmeg.

Drop each fillet into the melted butter and grill, with the grill set as high as possible over the coals. The salmon should smoke as well as cook. Remove and let cool a bit if serving immediately. If serving cold, it should be refrigerated for at least 2 hours. To serve, spoon a mound of the ricotta on each plate and top with a piece of salmon. Serves 6 to 8.

Spinach

New England Salmon

After John Adams signed the Declaration of Independence, he wrote to his wife Abigail that the day of the signing would be the great epoch in the history of America: "It will be celebrated by succeeding generations as the great anniversary festival. It will be solemnized with pomp and parades, with shows, games, sports, guns, bells, bonfires and illuminations from one end of the continent to the other from this time forward, forevermore."

After he became president, the Adamses celebrated the festival by serving a traditional New England dinner of salmon with egg sauce, along with the first new potatoes and early peas.

They were living in Philadelphia in 1797 and she wrote to her sister about the celebration she had planned. She stated that the Fourth of July would be a most tedious day, as they must have not only served all of the Congress, but also the gentlemen of the city, the governor with his officers and companies. The house would not hold all of the guests, so long tables were to be set up in the yard.

Abigail also mentioned that when President Washington celebrated the Fourth of July, he only served cake, punch and wine. But since her husband was now president and they were in Philadelphia, they could not afford the trouble and expense so they would serve a traditional New England dinner. All the foods needed could be supplied locally and at moderate expense.

New England Poached Salmon with Egg Sauce

To poach salmon: Take a whole salmon or a 4- to 5-pound piece from the center of the fish. Wash the salmon and then wrap it in cheesecloth, leaving long ends to help lift it from the poaching liquid. Bring 2 to 3 quarts of salted water to a boil. The amount will vary due to the size of the fish. Add 3 or 4 peppercorns, a bay leaf and 3 or 4 slices of lemon. Bring to a boil for at least 15 minutes. Reduce to a simmer and add the fish. Cook for 6 to 8 minutes per pound or until the fish flakes; do not overcook. When the salmon is done, lift it from the broth and remove the cheesecloth. Place on a warm platter and remove skin very carefully. Garnish with lemon slices and parsley. While the salmon is cooking, make Egg Sauce.

Egg Sauce

1 cup milk
1 cup light cream
2 small onions, sliced
1/2 bay leaf

Salmon

New England Salmon (cont.)

Chapter

6

Gifts from the Sea

1 whole clove

3 tablespoons butter

3 tablespoons flour

1 teaspoon salt

White pepper

2 hard-cooked eggs, coarsely chopped

Heat the milk and cream with the onion slices, bay leaf and clove until a film forms; skim surface. In a saucepan, melt the butter; add the flour, stirring to keep it smooth, but do not let it brown. Pour in milk mixture and cook over low heat, stirring constantly until mixture bubbles. Remove from heat, season with salt and pepper, then strain into a saucepan. Add eggs and heat through, but do not cook any further. Thin with warm cream, if needed. Serve separately in a warm sauceboat. Makes 8 to 10 servings.

Salmon

A HOLIDAY FEAST

CHAPTER 6

Gifts from the Sea

Oysters have long been included in holiday feasts in towns near the coast. But thanks to modern refrigeration and transportation, they are now available everywhere.

Some dishes made from oysters were traditionally served in the White House by most of our presidents. They were served raw, stewed, baked or in a soup.

Mrs. Theodore Roosevelt always gave a party on Christmas Eve for the president's official family. The president always served Creamed Oysters. You might try this simple, traditional Christmas Eve dish this year under much less frantic circumstances than in Edith Roosevelt's time.

CREAMED OYSTERS

2 tablespoons butter

2 tablespoons flour

1 pint oysters

Oyster liquid

1/2 teaspoon Worcestershire sauce or
    lemon juice or sherry

Salt and paprika

Buttered toast

Melt the butter in a saucepan; add flour. Stir until blended. Drain the oysters and stir in oyster liquid. If it does not measure to 1 cup, add cream to make 1 cup. Stir constantly and add salt and paprika to taste. When the sauce is almost to a boil, add oysters; cook until sauce almost comes to boil again. Add Worcestershire sauce or lemon juice or sherry. Serve over buttered toast or, if you want it a bit fancier, serve in a patty shell. Garnish with chopped parsley. Serves 4.

Oyster

Tuna and More Tuna

Chapter 6

Gifts from the Sea

Man has been dining on tuna since prehistoric times. Tuna bones have been found in the ruins of kitchens dating from Upper Paleolithic to Iron Age times. Homer wrote that in his day, it was a favorite food of the Greeks. The tuna image appeared on Byzantine coins. Even the cities of Tunis, Tripoli and Syracuse began as "tinnoscopes," tuna observation centers manned by fishermen who would track the tuna migration from towers on the coastal cities.

In the Americas, tunas spawn in the warmer southern waters where they fatten up on herring and squid. Tuna season opens in June but the fish are at their best when taken from northern waters in late summer or early fall. The tuna is a warm-blooded fish with great endurance and speed. In order for the tuna to maintain a sufficient oxygen supply, it has to move through the water at a rate of 20 to 30 knots. They have been clocked at 45 miles per hour.

There are six major species of tuna, each with its own unique color, texture and flavor. Only four of these you are apt to find in our markets.

Albacore: This is the fish that provides most of the premium canned tuna. It is delicious poached or cut into steaks and grilled.

Bluefin: This is the largest tuna, averaging 3 to 6 feet in length, and weighing an average 400 to 600 pounds. It is dark in color with a decisive flavor which makes it preferred for sushi. It bears a resemblance to beef.

Bonita: A small fish with a silvery body and a steel-blue back with slanting dark-blue stripes, this fish's dark flesh has a strong flavor and cannot be labeled "tuna" by the American industry.

Yellowfin: A small tuna with an average weight of 20 to 30 pounds, it is a fine eating fish with flesh that is darker than that of albacore but lighter than that of bluefin.

This recipe for Pan-Blackened Tuna is one that may be cooked on a barbecue grill. I have found, however, that pan-blackening generates a great deal of smoke. If you want to avoid smoking up the kitchen, it is best to try the outdoor procedure, heating the pan on your grill. Serves 4.

Fish

TUNA AND MORE TUNA (CONT.)

6
CHAPTER

*Gifts from
the Sea*

PAN-BLACKENED TUNA

4 tuna steaks (about 6 ounces each), cut
    1/2-inch thick

1 stick (1/2 cup) butter, clarified

1 tablespoon salt

1 tablespoon garlic powder

1 tablespoon onion powder

1 tablespoon dried oregano

1 tablespoon paprika

2 teaspoons freshly ground black pepper

2 teaspoons fresh white pepper

2 teaspoons dried thyme

1/2 teaspoon cayenne

Lemon wedges for garnish

Trim the tuna to remove any skin or
darkened pieces. Clarify the butter. Combine
the butter, salt, garlic powder, onion powder,
oregano, paprika, peppers, thyme and cayenne.
Generously coat both sides of fish with the
spice mixture. (You may not need all the spice
mixture.) Cook the steaks in the super-hot
skillet for 1 to 1 1/2 minutes per side. Ignore
the smoke. Transfer to a platter and garnish
with lemon wedges.

Fish

A Spicy Shrimp Gumbo

6

Chapter

Gifts from the Sea

The most diverse group of spices we use belongs to the laurel family. The three are bay leaf, cinnamon and sassafras. Each comes from different parts of the world.

The bay leaf, a native to the Mediterranean area, was so loved by the Greeks and Romans they used its leaves to crown emperors and honor countrymen. The bay leaf used as an herb should not be confused with common laurel, which is poisonous.

Cinnamon is native to Sri Lanka and Southeast Asia. Its sweetness and warmth made it one of the most sought-after spices of the world. Most of the early voyagers went out looking for gold, but settled for cinnamon.

The eastern part of the United States produces a third of these two spices.

Sassafras is a relative newcomer to the spice world and is one of the few existing spices native to the United States. The aromatic leaves of the sassafras tree are dried and powdered to form file powder, a spice used in or with the lively Creole dishes from America's deep south. The powder sends out a mild flavor and is used primarily as a thickener stirred into the dish just before serving. Avoid boiling the mixture once the powder is added or the texture of the dish will be ruined. Many cooks sprinkle it on just as it is served. This recipe for Shrimp Gumbo will create a feast for the senses.

Shrimp Gumbo

4 tablespoons unsalted butter
1/4 cup flour
2 cups onion, chopped
1 cup chopped celery
1 1/2 cups chopped green pepper
1 clove garlic, minced
1 cup ham, cut in strips 1x1/2 inches wide
6 cups fish stock
1 can (28 ounces) tomatoes, chopped
1 1/2 teaspoons fresh thyme or 1/2 teaspoon dried, and crushed
1 1/2 teaspoons fresh oregano or 1/2 teaspoon dried and crushed
1/2 teaspoon cayenne
1 bay leaf
Salt to taste

2 packages (10 ounces each) okra
1 1/2 pounds shrimp, shelled
2 teaspoons gumbo *file* (sassafras)

In a large saucepan over moderate heat, melt the butter. Add the flour and cook, whisking until slightly browned. Add the onion, celery, green pepper, garlic and ham strips. Cook until onion is soft. Add fish stock, tomatoes, thyme, oregano, cayenne, bay leaf and salt to taste. Simmer mixture, stirring occasionally, for 1 hour.

Bring the mixture to a boil; add okra, cut into pieces. Reduce heat and simmer a few minutes or until okra is cooked. Add the shrimp and simmer until it is pink, about 2 minutes. Remove from heat; stir in the *file* powder. Let stand covered for 10 minutes. Serve on a bed of rice. Serves 6 to 8.

Onion

A Summer Favorite

Summer meals call for cool snacks, appetizers and drinks—something you can make ahead of time. Here is one of my favorite dishes for summer parties.

CHAPTER 6

Gifts from the Sea

Shrimp Remoulade

9 cups water

1 small onion

1 stalk celery

1 bay leaf

3 whole peppercorns

3 pounds unpeeled fresh shrimp

3/4 cup oil

1/2 cup horseradish mustard

1/3 cup tarragon vinegar

1 cup minced celery

1/4 cup chopped parsley

1 hard-cooked egg, chopped

2 teaspoons chopped green onion

1 teaspoon salt

2 teaspoons paprika

Dash Tabasco

Lettuce leaves

Lemon wedges

Combine the water, onion, celery, bay leaf, and peppercorns in a large kettle; bring to a boil. Add the shrimp and return to a boil. Reduce heat and simmer for 3 minutes. Drain well; cool in cold water. Peel and devein shrimp.

In a large bowl, combine the oil, mustard, vinegar, celery, parsley, egg, green onion, salt, paprika, and Tabasco; mix well. Add shrimp and toss. Cover and chill overnight or at least 8 hours. Serve in a lettuce-lined bowl, garnished with lemon wedges. Makes 10 to 12 servings.

Lemons

FOR THE BARBECUE

CHAPTER 6

Gifts from the Sea

Summer is the time to enjoy the excitement of aromatic, charcoal-grilled meat or fish covered with a tangy sauce. The grill may be one specially built or bought for the back yard, or a portable one for the terrace or canyon.

When choosing a spot for your barbecue, select a location away from overhanging trees and not on the grass. If located on flagstone or concrete, some of the grease or marinade could splatter. Some store-bought kitty litter sprinkled on the stone or concrete will absorb any drippings.

Start your fire at least 45 minutes before cooking to give the charcoal time to stop burning and become red and glowing. Cooking times will vary depending on the heat of the coals. Spit cooking takes longer, since you are usually cooking larger pieces of meat or fowl.

Fish should be cooked with a slightly higher temperature. When cooking fish, a fine-meshed grid or fish basket will prevent it from splitting its skin. Grill for 10 to 15 minutes, turning frequently and brushing with oil and lemon juice.

When grilling or spit roasting, allow larger pieces to come to room temperature before brushing with the marinade or sauces. The meat will absorb the flavors better if it is warm. Some special effects may be added by flavoring the coals. A clove of garlic cut in half and tossed on the coals when cooking steak or lamb will lend a subtle flavor. When cooking pork or ham on a spit, wait until it is almost done, then drop a spiral of orange or lemon peel in the fire for a great aroma. A pinch of dry herbs sprinkled on the coals will burn immediately and give a delicious flavor to lamb chops.

This recipe is for barbecued halibut, but may be used for most fish steaks. Be sure to use a fine mesh grid or a fish basket to prevent the fish from breaking when turned.

BARBECUED HALIBUT STEAKS

4 halibut steaks, 1/2-inch thick,
7 ounces each

Salt and black pepper

4 tablespoons olive oil

2 tablespoons lemon juice

SAUCE

3 tablespoons olive oil

3 tablespoons butter

1 green pepper, cored, and chopped

1 medium onion, chopped fine

1 cup ketchup

2 cloves garlic, minced

2 bay leaves, crumbled

Salt and black pepper

Gridiron

For the Barbecue (cont.)

Mix the olive oil and lemon juice with some salt and pepper. Place steaks in a zip-bag and pour the mixture over them. Marinate for 2 hours in the refrigerator, turning several times.

Prepare the sauce in advance. In a large skillet, heat the oil with the butter and add the green pepper and onion. Saute till soft. Add ketchup, garlic and bay leaves. Season to taste with salt and pepper. Simmer for 10 minutes. Pour into saucepan that can be reheated on the grill.

When the coals are ready, remove the fish from its marinade and brush with marinade and sauce. Place fish on a fine-meshed grid or fish grid. Cook over hot coals 8 to 10 minutes, turning once. Heat the sauce while the fish cooks. Transfer to a warm platter and garnish with sauce. Pass any extra sauce separately. Serves 4 to 6.

6

Chapter

Gifts from the Sea

Gridiron

TRUE BUERRE BLANC WITH TURBOT

CHAPTER 6

Gifts from the Sea

Buerre blanc is not, strictly speaking, a classic sauce. It is, however, a classic of the regional cuisine of the west of France. Today it is served in most French restaurants and bistros. This housewife specialty has become a spe'cialite' de la maison.

When I was going to cooking school I asked the chef if I could make a sauce buerre blanc? He looked at me and said, "I know where you went to dinner last night." He mentioned a small restaurant that was located close to my apartment. I told him he was correct. He said that it was very nice, but I should preserve the memory of the sauce because it would be impossible to reproduce it. I had a challenge and returned to the restaurant and asked about the sauce. The waiter took me to the kitchen and introduced me to the chef. She said that she could not tell me how to make it but I could watch her. I rushed home and started to make it. To my surprise it turned out. I couldn't wait to try it on a friend. Luck was with me for Pat Shea, an old family friend, was in town for a little R&R from his studies at Oxford. He came over with a fellow classmate and we enjoyed my newly mastered sauce with turbot.

BUERRE BLANC

2 tablespoons shallots, finely chopped

1/4 teaspoon white pepper

1/2 teaspoon salt

1/2 cup white wine vinegar

3 to 6 sticks unsalted butter, chilled

1-1/2 tablespoons juice from the fish

Combine 1 tablespoon of the shallots, white pepper, salt, vinegar, and the juice that has collected in the small saucepan where the turbot is waiting to be poached. Reduce sauce by 3/4. Do not under reduce. The final reduction must be as acid as possible without boiling away. Remove from the heat and strain into a clean, heavy, non aluminum saucepan.

Crush the remaining shallots with the flat side of a heavy knife and add them to the reduction. Set the pan over very low heat. Then add 4 pats of butter and whisk. As soon as the first pats are melted, add 4 more pats. Continue in this manner until you have added all but 1 stick of butter. All the while you have to continue whisking, adding butter as it is melted. Remove from the heat and add the remaining stick of butter. correct for seasoning. Serve immediately over turbot which has been poached in a simple fish stock. Do not let the sauce cool or it will fall apart. Do not stop to answer the telephone!

Butter Boat

7

CHAPTER

Vegetables

Asparagus

Tomato

Potato

Artichoke

The Mystery of Asparagus

Chapter 7

Vegetables

Of all the familiar vegetables, few have histories less well-documented than asparagus. Its place of origin is unknown. In the 17th century, it was known in France but not introduced in England until a century later. Asparagus must have been deliberately brought to the United States. We know that Thomas Jefferson grew it from imported seeds, but not until after it had been mentioned in an American garden book in 1775.

Cultivated asparagus has been a luxury vegetable throughout its history. Ancient Egyptians cultivated spears and considered it a worthy offering to their gods. Jean de la Quintinie grew it in hotbeds, to assure Louis XIV of a year-round supply. As late as the Gay '90s in the U.S., when ostentatiously costly dinners were served in famous establishments like Delmonico's, Sherry's and the Waldorf-Astoria, a banquet at the Waldorf included fresh asparagus in February, evoking the comment that it was "an extravagant rarity."

The story is told that the French encyclopedist Bernard de Fontenelle was surprised by an unexpected visit from the Abbe Terrasson, who asked if he might stay for dinner. Assenting grudgingly and grumbling that he would be deprived of half of his favorite asparagus, de Fontenelle ordered the abbe's half be served with a white sauce the churchman liked and his half be served with an oil dressing he preferred. When, just before dinner, the Abbe suddenly rolled on the floor, stricken with apoplexy, de Fontenelle rushed to the kitchen and shouted, "All the asparagus with oil."

This recipe for fresh asparagus may be served to friends and family without fear.

Fresh Asparagus with Quick Barley

1 pound asparagus

1 shallot, minced

2 tablespoons butter, melted

1 cup quick barley

1/2 cup dry white wine

3 cups chicken broth

3/4 cup heavy cream

1/4 cup grated Parmesan cheese

1 clove garlic, minced

1/2 teaspoon pepper

1/2 teaspoon salt

1/2 cup pecans, toasted and chopped

Snap off the tough ends of the asparagus and discard. Remove the scales with a peeler. Cut off the tips and set aside. Thinly slice stems lengthwise.

Saute the shallots in the butter in a large skillet over medium heat. Add the barley. Stir in the wine and cook until the liquid has evaporated. Add the asparagus stems and 1/2 cup broth. Stir until the liquid is absorbed.

Asparagus

The Mystery of Asparagus (cont.)

Chapter 7

Vegetables

Continue adding the broth, a half cup at a time, stirring until the barley is tender. Stir in the heavy cream, Parmesan, garlic, salt and pepper. Cook a few minutes or until thick. Add asparagus tips and the pecans. Cook a minute and remove from heat. Let stand 5 minutes before serving. Serves 8.

Baked Asparagus

1 1/2 pounds fresh asparagus
2 tablespoons cucumber, peeled, seeded
    and cut in fine match-sticks
1/4 cup butter, melted
1/2 cup sliced almonds
1 tablespoon lemon juice
1 cup dairy sour cream or creme fraiche
1 tablespoon prepared horseradish
1/2 cup fresh bread crumbs
Sauce

Snap off tough ends of asparagus. Remove scales with a peeler. Cook in a small amount of water for 6 to 8 minutes, until tender crisp. Remove from heat; drain. Arrange asparagus in open buttered baking dish. Keep warm.

Cut cucumber into fine match-sticks; saute in skillet with melted butter and almonds. Add lemon juice; pour mixture over asparagus.

Mix sour cream and horseradish; pour over almond-cucumber layer. Sprinkle top with bread crumbs; dribble some melted butter over top. Bake at 350 degrees for 10 minutes or until top is brown. Makes 8 servings.

Asparagus

THE ANCIENT ARTICHOKE

CHAPTER 7

Vegetables

The Greeks and Romans devoured artichokes with gusto. And today they are about the most popular spring treat with the Italians and the French. The plant probably came to America with both French settlers in Louisiana and Spanish missionaries in California.

The artichoke was introduced in Florence from Naples, about 50 years before Catherine de Medici was born. In her time, it was her favorite food, especially when stuffed. This recipe has been adapted from Scappi's original.

STUFFED ARTICHOKE BOTTOMS

10 artichokes

Lemon juice

1/4 pound mushrooms, chopped

1 clove garlic, minced

1 small onion, minced

3 tablespoons butter or olive oil

2 tablespoons minced parsley

2 tablespoons lean minced ham
(prosciutto)

6 tablespoons grated Parmesan cheese

1 cup bread crumbs

Salt and pepper

1/3 cup diced mozzarella cheese

Cut stems of artichokes to level. Rub cut ends with lemon juice and cook in boiling salted water for at least 30 minutes or until tender. Discard leaves and fuzzy chokes and trim bottoms.

Saute mushrooms, garlic and onion in hot butter or oil or a mixture of the two until golden brown and dry. Mix with parsley, ham and 4 tablespoons grated cheese, bread crumbs, salt and pepper. Pack mixture in

mounds into each artichoke bottom. Top with a little mozzarella and sprinkle with remaining Parmesan. Pour a thin layer of olive oil into a shallow baking pan and arrange the bottoms, stuffed-side up, in a single layer. Bake in a 375-degree oven for about 20 minutes or until top is browned. Serve as a side dish with any meat or separately as an appetizer. Serves 5 to 10.

Artichoak

THE POPULAR POTATO

7

CHAPTER

Vegetables

The potato is undoubtedly the number one vegetable in the world. It did not become the important staple it is today until the mid 19th Century. Sir John Hawkins is credited with bringing the potato to England in 1563, but it was not cultivated and was re-introduced 20 years later by Sir Francis Drake.

Sir Walter Raleigh began growing potatoes on his estates in Ireland at about this same time. In France, the potato was regarded with great suspicion as late as 1770, when the chef August Parmentier popularized its use.

There are many ways of preparing potatoes. Some of the simplest are the best. One of the most popular is jacket-baked potatoes, served piping hot, cut open and filled with a pat of butter and sprinkled with salt and pepper. Another all-time favorite would be hash-browned potatoes that have been skinned and coarsely chopped, then slowly browned in butter and bacon drippings.

There are two potato crops: main crop or "old" potatoes and early or "new" potatoes. Some of these potatoes are better suited than others to particular purposes.

Try to select the right potato for the dish. The floury, mealy texture of the old potato is better used for baking, roasting, soups and purees. The firm waxy new potato is better suited for potato salad and dishes where it is important that the potato bits retain their shape. New potatoes are in season from May through September in most climates, but with modern transportation they may be available throughout the year—though at a price.

These new potatoes are most flavorful when very fresh. With this in mind, buy only the amount you need to use within 48 hours. They are best boiled or steamed; the larger ones make fine chips and saute superbly. It is not recommended that they be used for baking, roasting or pureeing.

The main crop or "old" potatoes are available from late September through the following May. When first harvested, their flesh may be waxy but will become floury during storage. They should be cooked with their jackets if possible, but if you do peel the raw potatoes, put them into water immediately to prevent them from discoloring. Do not allow them to remain in the water too long or they will lose some of their water-soluble nutrients.

A simple potato recipe I enjoy that only takes about an hour to prepare is a plain baked, individual potato loaf. A fancier dish is Gratin Dauphinois.

Potato

The Popular Potato (cont.)

Baked Potato Loaf (individual size)

1 1/2 pounds old potatoes
Salt and freshly ground pepper
4 tablespoons butter
3 tablespoons grated Parmesan cheese
2 large eggs
1 tablespoon dry bread crumbs

Peel potatoes and cut into even-sized cubes. Drop into pan of boiling salted water and cook about 20 minutes or until soft. Drain potato cubes and return to pan; toss over low heat until dry. Mash the potatoes or puree them in a processor. Add butter and 2 tablespoons of the cheese. Mix well and taste for seasoning.

Whisk one egg and beat into the potato mixture. Divide puree into 12 equal portions and form into a fat oval shape, then pat to loaf shape. With a sharp knife, cut diagonal slashes on top of each loaf. Transfer the little loaves to buttered baking sheets. Beat the remaining egg and brush top of each loaf. Mix the remaining cheese with bread crumbs and sprinkle on each loaf. Bake in pre-heated oven at 425 degrees for 20 minutes or until puffed and golden brown. Serve immediately.

Gratin Dauphinois

2 pounds large new potatoes
1 clove garlic
4 tablespoons butter
1 1/4 cups whipping cream
1/2 cup grated Swiss or Gruyere cheese
8 tablespoons grated Parmesan cheese
Salt and pepper to taste
Dash of nutmeg

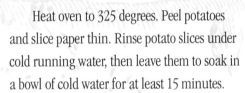

Heat oven to 325 degrees. Peel potatoes and slice paper thin. Rinse potato slices under cold running water, then leave them to soak in a bowl of cold water for at least 15 minutes.

Select a shallow ovenproof baking dish. Rub inside with a piece of cut garlic and then butter it thickly. Drain potatoes and dry with paper towel. Arrange a fourth of potato slices in overlapping rows in bottom of dish. Pour over at least 2 tablespoons cream and sprinkle with 2 tablespoons grated cheese and 1 tablespoon Parmesan. Season with salt, pepper and nutmeg. Continue to layer potatoes, cream and cheese, seasoning each layer with remaining ingredients. There should be about four layers. End with cheese and seasoning.

Bake at 325 degrees for 45 minutes, or until top is golden, bubbling, and potatoes are tender. If potatoes do not seem tender when tested with a skewer, cover dish with foil and cook for a few more minutes. Remove from oven and let settle for a few minutes before serving. Serves 8.

Potato

Zachary Taylor's Okra

CHAPTER 7

Vegetables

Zachary Taylor was one of the first presidents to become well acquainted with Creole cooking. He was elected president when he was 64 and his wife Margaret was 62. She was the most controversial thing about his short administration. After 38 years of following him from frontier post to frontier post and putting up with all the inconveniences, along with rearing six children, she was ready for a rest.

Social Washington did not like her because she did not entertain—nor did she even attempt it. She relegated all the official hostessing to her daughter Betty Bliss, wife of Maj. W.S. Bliss.

It is to Betty and her father that we owe a debt of gratitude for broadening the base of American cooking in his day. Not content to fall into the pattern of official Washington in serving standard Southern-New England-French fare, his administration introduced some of the Creole dishes that he had learned to love in Louisiana.

His favorite summer dish was fresh okra with tomatoes. Okra was originally imported from Africa to Louisiana, where it became a staple and a favorite when prepared with onions, bacon and tomatoes.

Okra with Tomatoes

1/2 cup chopped onion

1 pound okra, sliced

3 cups fresh tomatoes, chopped

1/2 teaspoon paprika

1 1/4 teaspoons salt

1/4 teaspoon curry powder

2 teaspoons brown sugar

Dash Worcestershire sauce

1 green pepper, chopped

1 clove garlic, minced

Heat bacon fat in heavy skillet. Add onion and saute lightly 4 or 5 minutes. Add okra and saute another 5 minutes. Add chopped tomatoes, paprika, and salt. Stir in curry powder, brown sugar and a dash of Worcestershire. Simmer for 10 minutes. Add green pepper and garlic. Cover and simmer until okra is tender. Serve hot. Makes 6 servings.

Tomato

STUFFED MUSHROOMS

Mushrooms have always been considered a delicacy and a classic garnish to many dishes. Mushrooms are the edible fruiting bodies of a group of leafless plants called fungi. The most highly prized of these is the truffle, an expensive and rare fungi most of us never use.

According to common folklore, mushrooms were thought to be the results of lightning bolts or thunder striking the ground. The Romans called them the "food of the gods" for their delicious flavor, which enhances most any dish to which they are added.

The main mushroom cultivated is in America. It is biporus, which is closely related to the field mushroom. These mushrooms are graded commercially according to their stage of development. Button mushrooms are small with a thick membrane still covering the gills. These are used for salads, pickling, garnishing and for soups and sauces that need to remain white. At the cup stage, the membrane has been broken to reveal the gills. These are used for fritters, garnishes, casseroles, soups or for stuffing as an hors d'oeuvre or a vegetable accompaniment. This stuffed mushroom recipe is one I particularly enjoy.

STUFFED MUSHROOMS

1 pound medium-size mushrooms

2 tablespoons butter

3 ounces cream cheese

1 ounce bleu cheese

2 tablespoons minced onion

1/4 teaspoon fine herbs

Quickly wash or brush the mushrooms; do not let them soak in water. Remove stems; chop fine. Melt butter in a skillet. When foaming subsides, add mushroom caps and saute over medium heat about 2 minutes. Remove from heat; cool.

Combine cream cheese, bleu cheese, mushroom stems, onion and fine herbs. Mix well; stuff mushroom caps with mixture. Dust with paprika and broil until bubbly. Serves 6.

Note: Fine herbs may be purchased or you may make your own by combining equal parts of minced parsley, chives, tarragon and chervil.

Mushrooms

THE VIDALIA ONION

CHAPTER 7
Vegetables

Vidalia onions are grown in 13 counties in southeast Georgia. In this region, the combination of loamy soil, mild weather and a 50-year tradition conspire to raise the lowly onion to the level of art. Because of the early season, these onions do not have time to develop a strong taste. Vidalias are protected by the closest thing America has to an appellation controlee: "Bootleggers" caught using the name Vidalia for onions grown outside the area can be fined up to $20,000.

These sweet onions are among the most fleeting of vegetables. Their season lasts only six to eight weeks from May until mid-June. They have a large proportion of water and 12.4 percent sugar.

BAKED VIDALIA ONIONS

4 large Vidalia onions
2 tablespoons butter
3 strips thick bacon
4 tablespoons cream cheese, room
   temperature
1 teaspoon Worcestershire sauce
Salt and black pepper

Beginning at the pointed end, core the onions almost through to the root side leaving the root intact to hold the onion together. Remove the skin. Place a bit of butter in each onion. Wrap tightly in foil and bake for about 20 minutes at 350 degrees. At this point, the onions should be starting to get soft.

Butter a baking dish just large enough to hold the onions. Cut bacon into slivers and fry until golden. Drain on a paper towel and set aside. In a bowl, beat cream cheese with Worcestershire and bacon bits. Take onions from the oven and remove foil. Stuff each onion with cheese mixture. Arrange in a baking dish and season with salt and pepper. Return to oven and bake for 15 to 20 minutes, or until onions are tender and cheese mixture is heated through. Serves 4.

Onions

TAILGATE ANTIPASTO

The air tingles with excitement as September greets the start of another football season. All this is just another reason to entertain. Whether the party is before or after or during the game, this vegetable dish should add to the occasion. It is easy to put together and is best served at room temperature.

This recipe is ideal when you have to furnish something special for a tailgate party. The entire dish can be made the night before and taken to the game in a plastic container.

CHAPTER 7

Vegetables

ROMAN VEGETABLE ANTIPASTO

3 small zucchini

1 stalk celery

1 cup green beans

2 or 3 small carrots

6 to 8 small button mushrooms

12 pearl onions

1/4 head cauliflower

1 green bell pepper

1 medium red bell pepper

1/2 small eggplant

5 tablespoons olive oil

1 clove garlic, quartered

1 bay leaf

Salt and black pepper

2 tablespoons dry white wine

2 tablespoons wine vinegar

1 tablespoon sugar

5 tablespoons ketchup

1/4 teaspoon lemon juice

Lettuce leaves, pitted black olives, tomato
     wedges for garnish

Cut zucchini and celery into slices. Cut green beans and carrots into 1-inch lengths. Wipe mushrooms and peel onions. Trim cauliflower into small florets. Cut peppers into squares. Slice eggplant; quarter each slice.

Heat olive oil in large heavy casserole dish. Add onions, eggplant, cauliflower, garlic and bay leaf. Season generously with salt and pepper. Toss to coat vegetables. Cover and simmer 10 minutes. Add celery and carrots; cover and simmer another 5 minutes. Add zucchini, beans and peppers; cover and simmer yet another 5 minutes.

In a bowl, combine wine, vinegar, sugar and ketchup. Stir this sauce into vegetables and add mushrooms and eggplant. Cover and simmer 10 minutes. Remove from heat and cool. Mix well but gently; chill. Before serving, taste for seasoning and add lemon juice. Place on a tray and garnish to serve. Sprinkle a bit of parsley over the top. Remove from refrigerator at least 1 hour before serving. Will keep well in refrigerator for several days.

Wine

The Hearty Leek

Chapter 7

Vegetables

The leek has been cultivated for as far back as our knowledge goes. Some writers claim it was native to the eastern Mediterranean.

The Irish claim it was in Ireland that St. Patrick transformed rushes to leeks to feed the sick to cure their illnesses.

Even though the Irish looked upon the vegetable as their own, they had rivals on the opposite shore of the Irish Sea.

The leek is the national emblem of Wales. On St. David's Day, Welchmen wear a bit of leek in their buttonholes in memory of the victory of King Cadwalader over the Saxons in A.D. 640. In this battle, the Welsh avoided going up against the wrong soldiers by wearing a leek in their caps as an identifying badge.

Today, the leek is one of our hardiest vegetables, which, wherever temperatures do not drop below 10 degrees, can be left in the ground all winter and will provide edible shoots and bulbs. They can be planted in the fall or winter and will survive the cold.

Despite its long history in the Mediterranean and Europe, the leek was not eaten much in America.

In postwar years, it has staged a comeback, with the aid of a new generation of young chefs who found original uses for it.

The Paris daily Le Monde referred to "the leek that hardly explored vegetable—which reserves for cooks of imagination some dazzling discoveries."

This recipe for leeks is Irish—with a touch of France—and developed by today's American chefs. You will enjoy it.

Leeks Mornay

8 medium-sized leeks

2 1/2 cups milk

2 or 3 slices carrot

2 or 3 slices onion

4 peppercorns

Sprig of parsley

2 tablespoons roux*

1 1/2 cups grated Cheddar cheese

1/4 teaspoon Dijon mustard

Salt and pepper

Buttered bread crumbs

*To make roux—mix 2 tablespoons flour with 2 tablespoons soft butter till smooth.

Trim most of the green part off the leeks. Leave the white part whole; slit the top. Wash well under cold running water. Cook in a little boiling salted water in a covered saucepan until just tender, about 15 minutes.

Saucepan

The Hearty Leek (cont.)

Chapter 7

Vegetables

Meanwhile, put milk into a saucepan with the sliced carrot and onion, peppercorns and a sprig of parsley. Bring to a boil, then simmer 5 minutes. Remove from the heat and leave to infuse for 10 minutes. Strain out the vegetables; bring back to a boil. Thicken with the roux. Do not let the roux brown. Let the milk thicken to a light coating consistency. Add mustard and two-thirds of the cheese. Season with salt and black pepper to taste.

Drain the leeks; arrange in a serving dish. Coat with the sauce and sprinkle with remaining cheese and buttered bread crumbs. Reheat in the oven at 350 degrees until golden and bubbly. Serves 8.

Saucepan

Fried Okra

Chapter 7

Vegetables

Okra was introduced to the Western hemisphere by black slaves from Africa, probably its place of origin. However, some votes are always cast for Asia.

Okra is tied to Africa by its name. It comes from nkrumum, from the Twi language spoken on the Gold Coast. Slaves from Angola called it Umbundu, which became "gumbo," originally referring to the vegetable. Now it is applied to the dish in which it is used most often—a stew that was originally thickened with file powder made from dried sassafras leaves. When okra appeared on the scene, it replaced the file as a thickener, thus contributing its original name to the stew. Today there are still traditionalists who prefer the powder as a thickener and you will find gumbos which have no okra in them. I am told you never use both unless you prefer a stew with the consistency of glue.

Okra is harvested unripe, when the pods are less than 9 inches long. If allowed to ripen, the pods become fibrous and indigestible. Today, it is used mostly in soups and stews. It is cut cross section into disks that look like little wheels with the seeds nestled between the spokes. The taste is pleasing, a little tart and crisp.

Okra's outstanding feature is that it is mucilaginous, which makes it a good thickener. It is used in a number of ways. It is often cooked like asparagus and pickled. A side dish of okra is made by combining fresh tomatoes with fresh corn, chopped onion, chopped celery, salt and pepper, and simmering the mixture until the okra is tender.

My friend, Ellen Furgis, a truly great cook, serves it fried. This recipe for Fried Okra may not be her exact recipe, but is one I concocted with good results.

Fried Okra

> 4 cups sliced okra
> 1/4 teaspoon salt
> 1/4 teaspoon pepper
> 1 cup buttermilk
> 3/4 cup cornmeal
> 1/4 cup flour

Wash and drain okra. Cut off the tip and stem end and cut into 1-inch slices. Sprinkle okra with salt and pepper. In a shallow dish, combine it with the buttermilk. Let stand for about an hour or until most of the milk is absorbed. Mix the cornmeal and flour together and dredge the okra. Fry in deep hot oil (375 degrees) until golden brown. Drain on a paper towel. Transfer to a serving platter and serve hot. Produces 4 to 6 servings.

Chapter 8

Breakfast, Brunch & Pancakes

Egg

Pig

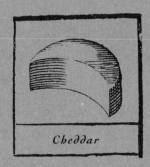

Cheddar

Batter Pitcher

The Hard Boiled Egg

The first and most important rule when using eggs is that they should not be boiled, but simmered. Boiling gives eggs a rubbery texture. If your eggs are kept in the refrigerator, take them out in plenty of time so they come to room temperature before cooking. This should prevent the shells from cracking while cooking. Pierce the broad end of the egg with a pin or use an egg prick—a little gadget made just for this. This little hole releases the pressure caused by the increased temperature of the water.

There are several methods of hard-cooking eggs. Some people prefer to start the eggs in boiling water, while others prefer to start with cold water. The method I use most often for hard-cooked eggs is to place them in a saucepan and cover with cold water. Let the water come to a boil and cover with a lid. Reduce the heat to a slow simmer, or even turn the heat off and let the eggs rest in the hot water for 8 to 10 minutes. Larger eggs take more time to cook. When they have cooked for the correct time, plunge them into cold water and leave them until they are cold. Soft-cooked eggs are only left in for 3 to 4 minutes and are not chilled in cold water. Try not to overcook hard-cooked eggs. Overcooking causes the surface of the yolk, where it meets the white, to turn a green-black color.

Plunging the hard-cooked eggs into cold water not only prevents further cooking but shrinks the inner membrane away from the shell and makes them easier to peel. Older eggs are much easier to peel than fresh ones. When eggs are cold, gently tap to crack the shell. Roll the egg between your hands until the shell starts to break away then gently peel the shell away.

One of my favorite hard-cooked egg dishes is Hot Curried Eggs, served with boiled rice.

Hot Curried Eggs

6 large eggs, hard-cooked

2 tablespoons butter

1/2 cup minced onion

1 1/2 tablespoons flour

2 teaspoons curry powder

2 cups chicken stock

4 tablespoons heavy cream

1 teaspoon chutney (avoid any pieces)

Salt and pepper

A few drops lemon juice

2 cups boiled rice

1 tablespoon minced parsley

Shell eggs and cut them in half lengthwise. In a saucepan, melt the butter and saute the onion until soft and slightly golden. Stir in the flour and curry powder and cook for

Egg

Chapter

8

Breakfast, Brunch & Pancakes

a couple of minutes. Gradually add the stock; whisk vigorously to prevent lumps. Bring to a boil, then simmer uncovered for 30 minutes, stirring constantly. Remove from heat and beat in whipping cream and chutney. Season to taste with the salt, pepper and lemon juice. Fold the halved hard-cooked eggs into the sauce; return the pan to heat and heat thoroughly for 3 or 4 minutes. Serve eggs on a bed of hot boiled rice, garnished with parsley. Makes 6 servings.

Egg

The Incredible Egg

After any period of excessive eating (holidays, vacations, etc.) it is always nice to return to simple cookery. Nothing better could be found than the incredible edible egg. Scrambled eggs, called oeufs brouilles in France, may not command the skill of making an omelette, but in their own simple way require care and attention. They make a surprisingly rich little dish. I did find that 2 eggs per person plus 1 for the pan are ample.

CHAPTER 8

Breakfast, Brunch & Pancakes

Scrambled Eggs for Four

9 large eggs

Salt and black pepper to taste

4 tablespoons cream or water

4 tablespoons butter

1 teaspoon mayonnaise

Break the fresh eggs, at room temperature, into a bowl, then stir with a fork until the yolks and whites are mixed. Never "beat" the eggs, as this will introduce air into the mixture and the eggs will not achieve a smooth, creamy texture. Stir in seasoning and some cream or water, allowing 1 tablespoon for every 2 eggs, not counting the one for the pan. Water breeds a fluffy scrambled egg while cream gives a richer, smoother texture.

The pan used should be a heavy skillet or saucepan. Heat butter before adding egg mixture. The depth of the liquid eggs should not be more than 1 inch so that the heat will permeate all eggs evenly. The mixture should be cooked over low heat and stirred so the eggs thicken gradually and smoothly. It is a good idea to remove the pan from the heat a few seconds before the eggs are scrambled to your liking. At this point, add a teaspoon of mayonnaise and stir in. This keeps the eggs shiny and smooth. They may be served plain or on toast, in pastry shells, hollowed-out rolls or on fried croustades.

Some of the mouth-watering variations for the plain scrambled eggs you could try are the following: any ingredients should be added just before serving: 6 ounces smoked salmon tossed in hot butter; 6 button mushrooms, sliced and sauteed in butter; 2 ounces fresh Parmesan cheese; 2 ounces grated Gruyere or 4 ounces grated cheddar cheese.

Saltbox

Understanding the Omelette

Chapter 8

Breakfast, Brunch & Pancakes

So much has been said as well as written about the omelette's capricious nature that otherwise daring cooks often refuse to attempt it. In actual fact, most of omelette making is easier to do than explain.

Small omelettes are easier to make than big ones. Four eggs will produce an omelette for 3 or 4 people. If you have more guests, it is best to make several, for then they arrive at the table hotter and maintain a better consistency.

Some cooks claim that an omelette can be made in any pan. I, however, keep a pan designed exclusively for eggs and omelettes—one of good weight, with rounded sides so the eggs can slide easily onto a plate when cooked. Unless you want your omelette to stick, never wash the pan. Instead, just rub it clean with a paper towel and a few drops of oil. A pan about 7 to 8 inches in diameter is just about right for a 4-egg omelette

Practice makes perfect, and once you have mastered the basic omelette you are ready to try any of the many variations. I will coach you through a basic recipe and then provide some variations.

For a small omelette, break 4 eggs into a bowl; season with salt and pepper to taste. If desired, you may add a tablespoon of water or cream. Heat the pan on medium heat until the butter sizzles on contact. Beat the eggs with a fork or whisk for a few seconds, just enough to mix the yolks and whites. Add a tablespoon of butter to the pan and shake it so the butter coats the bottom evenly. When the butter is sizzling—but has not changed color—pour the eggs in all at once.

Quickly stir the eggs for a second or so, so that they are cooking evenly, like you would for scrambled eggs. As the eggs start to set, lift the edges with your fork so the liquid can run underneath. Repeat until the liquid is all used up but the eggs are still soft and moist. You can slip the eggs in the pan by shaking the pan during this operation.

Now, remove the pan from the heat and, with one movement, press the handle downward and slide the omelette toward the handle. When a third of the omelette has slid up the rounded edges of the pan, fold this quickly toward the center with a knife. Now raise the handle and slide the opposite edge of the omelette one-third up the side farthest away from the handle. Hold a heated serving plate under the pan and as the rim of the omelette touches the plate, raise the handle more and more until the pan is upside down. Quickly finish the omelette by skimming a piece of butter over the surface to leave a glistening trail.

Laying Hen

UNDERSTANDING THE OMELETTE (CONT.)

Some of the most delicious omelettes are the easiest to prepare, but remember to make the filling before you make the omelette itself.

Just before the eggs are beginning to set, add any of these variations: 2 tablespoons freshly grated cheese; 2 tablespoons finely minced watercress; 4 tablespoons diced boiled potatoes browned in butter with 1/2 teaspoon chopped parsley and 1/2 teaspoon chopped chives. Or for a mushroom omelette, marinate 1/4 pound sliced mushrooms in 1 tablespoon brandy for 15 minutes. Add to a saucepan with 1 tablespoon butter and heat until moisture has evaporated. Add 2 tablespoons heavy cream, salt and pepper to taste. Keep warm until ready to add to omelette.

CHAPTER 8

Breakfast, Brunch & Pancakes

Laying Hen

The French Omelette

8

Chapter

Breakfast, Brunch & Pancakes

If my explanation for making a classic omelette was a little too complicated, I apologize. To make up for this, try making a perfect flat omelette, golden on both sides and filled with delicious little extras.

There are two ways of making flat omelettes. In Spain and Italy all the ingredients are cooked together in the same way. For a Spanish tortilla or an Italian frittata, the filling of onion, bacon or sausage and thinly sliced vegetables—usually potatoes or green beans— is sauteed separately in an iron frying pan. The lightly beaten eggs are poured over and then cooked. In France, on the other hand, the filling is cooked in one pan and the omelette in another. The filling is added just as the eggs begin to set on the bottom. I think the French version is easier, as sometimes the acids in the meat and vegetable filling in the frittata and tortilla tend to make them stick to the pan. The results, either way, will be delicious.

Flat omelettes are mostly served hot, direct from the pan, yet there is no reason that they could not be served cold. The Spanish serve a wedge of tortilla with drinks. In France the omelette sometimes is rolled up and put into a hollowed-out loaf of bread as a picnic food.

If you do not own a special omelette pan, you may use any heavy skillet that has an even base and a smooth, clean surface. The size of the pan is important. For a 2- or 3-egg omelette, use a 6-inch pan; for a 5- to 6-egg omelette, use a 7- to 8-inch pan; and for 8 eggs, use a 9-inch pan.

To assure a perfect omelette, the eggs and butter have to be of the very best quality. For each flat omelette break the eggs into a bowl and season with salt and pepper. A tablespoon of water or milk may be added at this point. Beat with a fork or whisk for about 30 seconds or just enough to mix the whites and yolks. Heat the pan over medium heat and add the butter. While butter is melting, shake the pan so bottom is evenly coated. Do not let the butter burn. Pour the eggs into pan all at once. Quickly stir the eggs just as you would for scrambled eggs. As the eggs start to set, lift the edge in several places so that the liquid egg can run under. Continue this until no liquid is left but the eggs are still moist. Shake the pan to make sure the omelette is not sticking. Spread any meat and vegetables that you are adding on the surface. Place a large plate over the top of the pan and turn the omelette out onto it, browned side up. Add a bit of butter to the pan and slide the omelette back into the pan to brown. Slip the completed omelette onto a warm plate. Take a bit of butter on the tip of a knife and glaze it. Garnish with parsley or watercress. Cut into wedges and serve. This recipe for a simple French flat omelette will take about 10 minutes to make.

Pig

THE FRENCH OMELETTE (CONT.)

Chapter 8
Breakfast, Brunch & Pancakes

FRENCH FLAT OMELETTE

    3 tablespoons butter
    6 ounces ham, cut into small cubes
    1 Spanish onion, thinly sliced
    Salt and pepper
    8 eggs
    Parsley, chopped for garnish

In a saucepan, melt a bit of butter; saute ham. Add onions and cook until soft. Season with salt and pepper; set aside and keep warm.

Add to flat omelette just before turning, as instructed above.

Pig

Happy New Year!

8

Chapter

Breakfast, Brunch & Pancakes

In our time, the most important holiday in January is New Year's Day. For many years in England, it was customary to clean house Jan. 1, a practice which survives metaphorically in our "cleaning the slate" to make New Year's resolutions. Jan. 2 is sacred to St. Macarius, the patron saint of pastry cooks. Other January holidays include Twelfth Night (Jan. 5), which marks the end of Christmas festivities, and Epiphany (Jan. 6), which honors the visit the Wise Men from the East made to the baby Jesus.

Bleu cheese has long been associated with January. It is most comforting to sit by a warm fire and nibble bleu cheese while sipping a fine port wine. The closest many people get to bleu cheese is in a salad dressing, which is unfortunate, because the bleus include three of the world's greatest cheeses: Stilton, Gorgonzola and Roquefort. Stilton is produced in only three counties in central England. Gorgonzola is Italy's answer to Stilton. Both of these cheeses are made from cow's milk. In France, the great bleu cheese is Roquefort, made from goat's milk. Most American bleu cheeses are made from cow's milk, and American bleu is now considered to be as good as the three imports. I recently received some American bleu from Iowa and class it equal to or better than the imported ones.

This recipe for a souffle will help use up any bleu cheese you may have left in your refrigerator. Do not be afraid of the recipe because it is a souffle. Three important points are: first, carefully butter the sides, bottom and rim of the souffle dish so the souffle can rise without obstruction; second, beat the egg whites to stiff but not dry consistency; and lastly, have the base mixture piping hot when you fold in the whites.

Bleu Cheese-Leek Souffle

4 ounces bleu cheese

2 leeks, chopped

5 tablespoons butter

1/3 cup fine bread crumbs

4 tablespoons flour

1 cup milk

4 egg yolks

Salt, pepper, cayenne, nutmeg

6 egg whites

Pinch of cream of tartar

Crumble the cheese into bits; set aside. Wash the leeks and finely chop. Melt the butter in a saucepan; brush bottom, sides and rim of a 5-cup souffle dish. Chill the dish for 30 minutes and brush with melted butter again. Coat inside of dish with bread crumbs. You should have about 3 tablespoons melted butter

Cheese

Happy New Year! (cont.)

8
Chapter
Breakfast, Brunch & Pancakes

left in the saucepan. Add the leeks to the saucepan and cook until tender. Stir in flour to make a roux. Remove from heat, whisk in milk; return to the heat for 2 to 3 minutes, stirring constantly. Reduce heat; beat in egg yolks, one at a time, removing from heat as soon as mixture thickens. Add bleu cheese, salt, pepper, cayenne, and nutmeg. Go easy on the salt, as the cheese is already quite salty. Season to taste.

Beat egg whites with a pinch of salt and cream of tartar until stiff. Stir one-fourth of the whites into the hot sauce. Fold the cheese sauce back into the whites; do not over fold. Pour this mixture into a souffle dish and smooth top with a wet spatula. Run your thumb around inside of dish to clear edges; wipe any spills off sides. Bake at 400 degrees for 20 to 30 minutes or until puffed and cooked. Serve at once. Remember, *guests* wait for the *souffle*, not the other way around.

Cheese

Parsnip Pancakes

Chapter 8

Breakfast, Brunch & Pancakes

The sturdy winter root vegetables are often considered the dregs of the vegetable world.

Children do not really like them, adults push them to the edge of their plates and even dogs have been known to reject them. Ogden Nash once called the parsnip "an anemic beet." In spite of all this, the parsnip, as humble as it may be, is remarkable in that it has a full earthy flavor and the best keeping qualities in winter. During World War II, the root saved thousands of Europeans from starvation.

The parsnip has a strange past. In England during the second century, it was thought to cause delirium and madness. In medieval Europe its sweetness made it the choice vegetable to serve with salted fish. Before the arrival of the potato in Europe, parsnips were the most common vegetable.

The ancient people of Europe dug them in the wild, but never cultivated them. They are best if left in the ground until after the first frost in that the cold helps convert the starches to sugar and makes them sweeter.

This recipe for Parsnip Pancakes has an Early American origin. It was originally flavored with sherry and sugar and served as a dessert. This recipe is for a vegetable side dish. Try it and you may become the first kid on your block to like parsnips.

Parsnip Pancakes

1 pound parsnips
2 eggs
1/2 cup flour
1/2 teaspoon baking powder
Salt, white pepper and nutmeg
3 tablespoons butter
3 tablespoons vegetable oil

Peel parsnips; cut into 1/2-inch slices. Cook in a steamer for 5 minutes or until soft. Drain and puree. Add eggs, flour, baking powder and a good pinch of salt, pepper and nutmeg.

Heat the butter and oil in a skillet over medium heat. Ladle the batter in 3-tablespoon batches to make a 3-inch pancake. Cook 2 minutes on each side or until browned. Add more oil and butter to pan and continue to cook pancakes. Serve hot. Serves 4 to 6.

DOLLAR PANCAKES

Some authorities claim it takes a maple tree 40 years to reach a 10-inch diameter—the size suitable for tapping. This explains the high cost of finished maple syrup.

Vermonters claim the worse the weather the better the sugaring. When the syrup comes from the evaporator, it is graded by density and color in accordance with strict standards established by the state. In Vermont, the highest grade is Vermont Fancy, distinguished by its light amber color and fine delicate flavor. In descending order come Grade A Medium Amber, Grade A Dark Amber and Grade C.

Unopened, maple syrup keeps indefinitely. Once opened, it should be refrigerated.

DOLLAR PANCAKES WITH MAPLE BUTTER

1 cup stone-ground cornmeal

1 cup flour

1 teaspoon baking soda

1 teaspoon baking powder

2/3 teaspoon salt

2 eggs

1 1/2 cups buttermilk

1 tablespoon maple syrup

4 tablespoons vegetable oil

3 tablespoons butter

Maple Butter

To prepare pancake batter, sift cornmeal, flour, baking soda, baking powder and salt. In a separate bowl, beat the eggs with 2/3 cup of the buttermilk, the maple syrup and 2 tablespoons of the oil. Whisk egg mixture into flour mixture, adding more buttermilk as needed to give batter the consistency of light whipped cream.

Heat 1 tablespoon of the remaining oil and 1 1/2 tablespoons butter on a griddle or skillet over medium heat. Drop the batter from a spoon into dollar-sized cakes. Cook on one side for about a minute or until bubbles appear. Turn and cook for another minute. Use the rest of the oil and butter to cook the remaining pancakes. Serve hot off the griddle with the Maple Butter.

MAPLE BUTTER

1 stick (1/2 cup) unsalted butter, room temperature

1/2 cup maple syrup

Cream the butter in a mixer. Gradually add maple syrup in a thin stream until well blended. This will keep for 3 weeks in the refrigerator.

Maple Bucket

Napoleon Would Approve

8

Chapter

Breakfast, Brunch & Pancakes

Artichokes are at their prime in April and one wonders if our forebears who learned to eat seemingly inedible foods were doing this on April Fools' Day. How could a person manage to eat a plant as tall as he with prickly leaves and a fruit with spiny petals? Of course, you wouldn't eat a raw choke, as the flesh is astringently bitter. Today, more artichokes are grown in California than in any other state. In Castroville, California, the self-proclaimed artichoke capital, some 50 billion pounds are harvested every year.

The most common way to enjoy artichokes is boiled or steamed, eaten petal by petal. With this recipe, you will be able to enjoy the petals and save the hearts for this variation on eggs Benedict. The eggs are served on fresh artichoke hearts and crowned with a bearnaise sauce instead of the usual hollandaise. The dish is named after Andre Massena, a general under Napoleon, the hero of the battle of Rivoli. Fresh tarragon is necessary.

Eggs Massena
(Poached Eggs with Artichokes)

4 large artichoke hearts, cooked
Bearnaise Sauce:
2/3 cup dry white wine
1/3 cup tarragon vinegar
3 tablespoons shallots, minced
2 tablespoons fresh tarragon, chopped
White pepper
1/2 cup unsalted butter
3 egg yolks
Salt and cayenne pepper
4 fresh eggs
1 tablespoon wine vinegar

To make the sauce, combine the wine, tarragon vinegar, shallots, 1 tablespoon fresh tarragon and 1/8 teaspoon white pepper in a heavy saucepan. Boil the mixture until only 3 tablespoons of liquid remain. Remove from heat and cool. Meanwhile, melt the butter and let it cool slightly. Add the egg yolks to the vinegar mixture, and cook over low heat, whisking constantly for 1 minute or until it becomes the consistency of mayonnaise. If the eggs start to scramble, remove them from heat and place in a bowl of cold water. Whisk the warm, melted butter into the wine mixture—the sauce will thicken. Whisk in the remaining tablespoon of chopped tarragon; add salt and cayenne and more white pepper to taste. The sauce is highly seasoned. Keep warm in a pan of hot water, not a double boiler.

Poach eggs 3 minutes in hot water with vinegar. Remove with a slotted spoon, trim edges, and keep warm in a pan of warm water. Heat the artichoke hearts in poaching water. Remove and blot dry. Spoon sauce into each heart. Put poached egg on top; spoon sauce over egg.

Artichoak

Mardi Gras Pancakes

The Romans held a purification rite during the last days of February which could be the predecessor of Christian Lent. Lent is a 40-day period of fasting and repentance to commemorate Jesus' six-week fast in the desert. In the Middle Ages, Lent was most rigorous; many foods were forbidden. Among these were butter, cheese, milk, eggs and meat. At the close of Lent on Easter Sunday, the eggs returned in their hard-boiled glory.

Today, many modern Christians limit themselves to giving up one cherished food. I, for instance, could easily give up rutabagas and spinach.

The fast officially begins on Ash Wednesday. For centuries in preparation of the fasting period, Christendom has indulged in pre-Lenten bashes that began the day after Christmas. This was called carne vale, or "farewell to meat," and the origin of our word carnival.

The parties and parades reach their peak on Shrove Tuesday, better known by its French name Mardi Gras, when all forbidden foods were consumed with abandon. Eggs were transformed into pancakes, which are still eaten in England on this day. All meats and fried foods are devoured in every form. Doughnuts and pancakes are the most common food served in modern America. A favorite pancake recipe uses maple syrup as the sweetener in the batter.

Mardi Gras Pancakes

1 cup white cornmeal
1 cup flour
1 teaspoon baking soda
1 teaspoon baking powder
1/2 teaspoon salt
2 eggs
1 to 1 1/2 cups buttermilk
1 tablespoon maple syrup
4 tablespoons oil
3 tablespoons butter

Mix the cornmeal, flour, baking soda, baking powder and salt in a large mixing bowl.

In a separate bowl, beat eggs with 2/3 cup buttermilk, the syrup and 2 tablespoons oil. Whisk the wet ingredients into the dry ones, adding more buttermilk, as needed.

Heat 1 tablespoon oil and 1 1/2 tablespoons butter in a skillet or griddle over medium heat. Use a large spoon to ladle batter on the griddle to make dollar-size pancakes. Cook about 1 minute or until bubbles appear on the surface. Turn, and cook one more minute. Use the rest of the oil and butter to cook remaining pancakes. Serve hot with syrup and butter. Serves 4 to 5.

Corn

Jewish Pancakes

8

Chapter

Breakfast, Brunch & Pancakes

Volumes have been written on the history of the potato. We know it originated in the Andes and was the mainstay of the Indian diet. The Spanish brought it to Spain during the 16th century. Northern Europeans, however, were not as enthusiastic about its use. For that matter, in Burgundy it was banned in 1619 because it was thought to cause leprosy.

The potato is today the world's largest vegetable crop, ranking fourth as a food crop after corn, wheat and rice. It is most versatile, for it can be baked, broiled, mashed, fried, made into pancakes and even ground into a flour.

At the beginning of Hanukkah, during these eight days of the Celebration of Light, most Jewish homes will traditionally feature latkes or potato pancakes. The oil used in them is symbolic of the oil used to light the Eternal Flame that lasted for eight days at the time of the victory of the Maccabees. I am sure that most Jewish families have a special family recipe they always use. My recipe was given to me by a Jewish friend a long time ago. Though some may question the use of a little baking powder, she felt it was a safety measure for a successful pancake. I feel the option is included only to assure a bit of leavening.

Latkes (potato pancakes)

3 cups grated potatoes

1/2 cup shredded onion

2 eggs, beaten

1 teaspoon salt

1/4 teaspoon white pepper

2 tablespoons flour

1/2 teaspoon baking powder, optional

1/2 to 3/4 cup vegetable oil or rendered chicken fat

Grate potatoes and onion with a food processor or the larger holes on a hand grater. Transfer to a colander and squeeze the mixture to press out as much liquid as possible. Place mixture into a large bowl; stir in eggs, salt, pepper, flour and baking powder.

Heat the oil in a heavy 10- to 12-inch frying pan. Drop two generous tablespoons of the potato mixture into the pan, flattening mixture with the back of a tablespoon so you have two cakes about 3 inches in diameter. Fry over medium heat for 4 to 5 minutes per side or until golden brown and crisp. Drain on a paper towel and keep warm in a slow oven.

Stir potato mixture before frying a new batch. If more oil is needed in the pan, add more. Serve hot with applesauce, quince compote or dairy sour cream on the side. Makes 6 to 8 servings.

Potato

CORN GRIDDLECAKES

Breakfast, Brunch & Pancakes

Corn, an American delicacy, has been cultivated in Central America for at least three centuries. Without it, the Pilgrims would never have survived their first winter in Plymouth.

For centuries, sweet corn on the cob was enjoyed solely by the Indians. The better crops were grown along the headwaters of the Susquehanna River. It was discovered by white men on an expedition against the Iroquois Indians in 1679. Benjamin Franklin called the roasted ears "a delicacy beyond expression." Today, it is a favorite at picnics and banquets alike.

Few vegetables are more botanically diverse. There are varieties that grow 2 feet tall, and others that grow 20 feet; the ears range in size from a few inches to 2 feet. Midwesterners prefer yellow corn; Southwesterners prefer sweet corn; Southerners eat sweet, white "shoepeg;" and in the rest of the nation and in Utah, we seem to favor "butter and sugar" corn, distinguished by its blend of yellow and white kernels.

Corn is among the most perishable of vegetables. From the moment it is picked, the sugar in the kernels begins to transform into starch. For this reason, it should be enjoyed the same day it is picked. Mark Twain even recommended installing the boiling kettle at the edge of the field.

When buying corn, look for ears with fresh, green husks and clean, dry silk. Always strip back a little of the husk; the kernels should be firm, even-sized and plump with milky juices. Don't worry if one end is marred by a worm hole (break it off and discard); the worms always prefer the most tender ears. The best corn is sold from pickup trucks or from stands along the roads in August.

To cook corn on the cob, do so as quickly as you can. Bring several quarts of water to a rolling boil with a pinch of salt. If you suspect the corn to be more than a day old, add a tablespoon of sugar. If the corn is fresh, add the husked corn to the boiling water and cook for 2 or 3 minutes. Older corn will take 5 to 6 minutes. Do not overcook.

There are lots of other ways to serve fresh corn than on the cob. One of my favorite fresh corn dishes is a sort of griddlecake, sometimes called Corn Dodgers. The sweetness of the corn combined with cornmeal begets a wonderful combination for almost any meal.

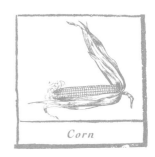

Corn

Corn Griddlecakes (cont.)

Chapter 8

8

Breakfast, Brunch & Pancakes

Fresh Corn Griddlecakes

1 cup flour

1 cup white cornmeal

1 tablespoon baking powder

1 tablespoon sugar

Pinch of salt

2 eggs, beaten

1/4 cup vegetable oil

1 cup buttermilk, approximately

3 ears fresh corn

4 tablespoons butter

Sift into mixing bowl the flour, cornmeal, baking powder, sugar and salt. Add eggs, oil and buttermilk; beat to mix. With a sharp knife, cut kernels off the cob. Stir into the batter. If the batter thickens too much, add more buttermilk.

Heat a griddle over medium heat and melt the butter. Spoon the batter onto the hot griddle to make 3-inch pancakes. Fry about 30 seconds on each side, turning once. Keep pancakes warm until all the batter has been used. Serve griddlecakes with syrup, jam or honey for breakfast, or with a dab of butter as a side dish for other meals. Makes about 12 to 14 griddlecakes.

Corn

A JEFFERSON FAVORITE

CHAPTER 8

Breakfast, Brunch & Pancakes

When Thomas Jefferson became president, he brought with him the great foods and wines of the world. His hospitality at Monticello was legend. Though he missed the dishes he had become accustomed to during his world travels, he always relished his plantation dishes. Still, he gave long lists of needed supplies to his friends and ministers to bring him when they returned from Europe to America.

In a letter from Jefferson to his traveling valet, Jefferson requested that he "bring a stock of macaroni, Parmesan cheese, figs, raisins, almonds, mustard, tarragon vinegar, oil and anchovies." Other gourmet presidents were to follow him in office—men such as Chester Arthur and William Howard Taft—but none ever challenged Jefferson as the greatest connoisseur of fine foods ever in the White House.

When he became president, Jefferson changed the name of the "President's Palace" to the "President's House." It actually was not called the White House until much later. His favorite meal was breakfast and his favorite dish was batter cakes. For this reason, he brought with him his Monticello cook, Annette, to Washington.

Jefferson's personal French chef was superb at making most everything else, but only a plantation-bred cook like Annette could make batter cakes just right. These were served often, and always for holidays such as Christmas, New Year's Day and the Fourth of July. Try this special holiday treat this season.

ANNETTE'S BATTER CAKES

4 tablespoons white cornmeal

1/2 teaspoon salt

2 cups milk

2 eggs, well beaten

Stir the cornmeal and salt into the milk and heat over medium heat for 5 minutes, stirring constantly. Cool. Add eggs and mix well. Heat a griddle that has been well greased to 375 degrees. Drop batter by the tablespoon and bake on one side until the cake is pocked with little holes. Turn only once. Do not stack, as the cakes are tender and will stick together. Serve with syrup or honey accompanied by sausage, bacon and fried apples. Makes 24 2-inch cakes.

Batter Pitcher

Fennel Pancakes

8
Chapter
Breakfast, Brunch & Pancakes

Fennel, generally harvested in the late fall and again in the spring, is available irregularly throughout the year. On the West Coast, it is grown year around. You should not plan a menu around it, but buy it when you find it.

In the 16th century, herbalist Thomas Tusser declared fennel an indispensable part of a garden. It is one of the nine holy herbs of the Anglo-Saxons. Shakespeare wrote of it. Fallstaff tells Poins that if fennel is eaten with eel, your sex life will be improved and assured. Taillevent, the royal chef, served it at a banquet given by Charles VI for the Count of Anjou in 1455. In England, it was in general use at least by the reign of Edward I in the 13th century. Italy regards fennel as a vegetable while France looks upon it as an herb.

In many French homes, the dried stems of the plant are placed on the coals to give flavor to grilled white fish. If you are looking for it in an Italian market, you should ask for finocchio. There are two types of fennel: a slender, flowering type grown for the leaves and seeds, and the bulbous variety, which is eaten as a vegetable. When buying fennel, look for compact bulbs: spreading leaves indicate overripeness and the center will be woody. The cut edges should appear fresh and the base should be free of brown spots.

This recipe is for a side dish that is served with fish or chicken. It is called a galette, referring to a crisp potato pancake. Do not soak the potatoes in water, as the starch is needed to hold the pancake together.

Fennel-Potato Galette

1 bulb of fennel
Salt
2 large potatoes
4 to 8 tablespoons butter
Black pepper

Wash and peel fennel and coarsely grate. Add fennel to a saucepan of rapidly boiling salted water. Blanch for less than a minute. Remove from the heat and refresh under cold water; drain.

Peel and grate potatoes. Add to the fennel and mix. In a large frying pan, heat half of the butter over medium heat. Add the fennel-potato mixture and pat into a pancake. Cook for 5 to 7 minutes per side, lowering the heat after 2 minutes to prevent the bottom from burning. Season both sides with salt and pepper. Remove to a warm plate. Add more butter to the pan, as needed, and cook the remaining pancakes. Serve warm with any fish or chicken dish. Serves 6 to 8.

Butter Boat

BLINY RUSSIAN PANCAKES

Chapter 8

Breakfast, Brunch & Pancakes

Since the first czar of Russia ruled in the ninth century, the cuisine of the land has always featured the use of plenty of fresh and soured cream. He came from what is today Sweden and introduced the rich cream sauces from his native land. The diet is not as lavish today as in the past, but it is still exciting because of its exotic flavors and combination of ingredients.

Modern-day Russians begin the day with cocoa or tea, buttered rolls and sometimes a boiled egg. Coffee was unknown until the Revolution of 1917, although it is commonly drunk today. The one food that has lasted through the years is Bliny, the famous buckwheat yeast pancake that was served long before Christianity came to Russia in the 19th century.

Originally prepared (or baked) as a symbolic golden offering to the Slav sun god, pancakes are now served on special occasions with their valuable commodity, caviar and sour cream. They are made with a mixture of plain flour and buckwheat flour for modern tastes. (If made entirely of buckwheat flour, they tend to be rather heavy.)

BLINY

1 cup all-purpose flour
1 teaspoon sugar
3 cups tepid milk
1 ounce (1 tablespoon) fresh or active dry yeast
2 eggs, separated
1/2 teaspoon salt
4 tablespoons heavy cream
3/4 cup buckwheat flour
Vegetable oil for grill
6 tablespoons butter

Mix half the all-purpose flour with the sugar; stir into 1/2 cup warm milk. Crumble the yeast into the mixture; blend well. Cover with a cloth and let mixture stand in warm place for 2 hours or until it is frothy.

Lightly beat egg yolks and add to yeast mixture along with salt, cream and remaining warm milk. Gradually add the rest of the flour and the buckwheat flour, stirring and beating. Whisk egg whites until stiff—but not dry—and fold into mixture. Cover with a cloth and let mixture rise in a warm place about 30 minutes. Beat batter down and let rise again. Repeat a third time.

Heat griddle and grease with vegetable oil. Dropping batter by the tablespoon on the hot surface, cook on one side for 2 or 3 minutes. Dribble uncooked side with melted butter and flip over. Cook another 2 minutes or until lightly browned. Serve hot with caviar or smoked fish and sour cream. Serves 6 to 8.

Batter Bowl

Buck Rarebit without the Buck

8

CHAPTER

Breakfast, Brunch & Pancakes

Traditionally, the spring season calls for the use of lots of cheese. Hard cheeses have long been celebrated for producing solid, well-flavored nourishment that traveled and lasted well. In modern America, all of them have a place on your cheese board, but they are also the cheeses most often used in cooking, to make a great range of exciting and nourishing dishes.

Cheddar is the best known of the hard cheeses, and the way of cheese-making called "cheddaring," which was developed before Tudor times on English west country farms, is now used worldwide. Parmesan, the pungent Italian grating cheese, has been famous for centuries as the finest cheese for seasoning. Swiss Emmental and Gruyere are prized for their melting qualities, and are now copied everywhere, perhaps most of all in the United States.

A delicious quick brunch recipe combines the use of eggs and cheese. When the poached eggs are used it is known as Buck Rarebit. Without the egg, it is just plain Rarebit.

Buck Rarebit

2 tablespoons butter

1 tablespoon flour

3 tablespoons milk

2 teaspoons dry mustard

2 tablespoons beer or ale

Dash of Worcestershire sauce

2/3 cup sharp Cheddar cheese, grated

Salt and fresh ground pepper

4 slices white bread, toasted

Butter

4 eggs, poached

Melt 2 tablespoons butter in saucepan. Stir in flour; cook slowly, stirring about 2 minutes. Do not let flour brown. Gradually stir in milk. Mix in mustard, beer and Worcestershire sauce.

Remove from heat; gradually add grated cheese, stirring until cheese is melted. Season to taste with salt and pepper.

Toast and butter the bread. Spread each slice with the rarebit. Put under the broiler and grill for about 2 minutes.

Meanwhile, poach eggs; drain well. Remove rarebit from oven; place a poached egg on each slice. Serve at once. Serves 4.

Cheddar

CHAPTER 9

Sweet Treats

Sugar Caster

Plum Pudding

Pine Apple

Apple

PRESIDENTIAL ENTERTAINING

CHAPTER 9

Sweet Treats

Martha and George Washington enjoyed entertaining and did so almost weekly at Mount Vernon and in the president's official home.

The couple hosted lavish parties in New York, Philadelphia and Washington (Federal City), wherever the Capitol happened to be. Mrs. Washington even published her own cookbook, "Rules for Cooking."

Expenses involved in running the presidential household were considerable. At this time, there was not an entertainment allowance for the president. The cost of his official entertainments came from his own pocket.

This may be the reason President Washington personally supervised the household accounts, keeping minute records of the daily use of all supplies. He spent more than $600 a month just for servants' wages and food; food for the presidential table cost $143 to $165 per week. There is little doubt that his presidential salary was more than used up during his term of office.

The holiday season was most important to the Washingtons, since they were married on Twelfth Night of 1759. Even during the war, Mrs. Washington traveled the icy winter roads with a special escort to spend the holiday with her husband.

One of the seasonal specialties served at Mount Vernon was Jumbles.

JUMBLES

3/4 cup butter

1 1/2 cups sugar

6 eggs; separated and beaten

1 tablespoon caraway seed

6 tablespoons rose water

6 tablespoons cream

Flour, as needed

1/2 teaspoon salt

Cream the butter well. Gradually add the sugar and the well-beaten yolks, then the beaten whites. Add the caraway seed, the rose water, cream and enough flour, sifted with salt, to make soft dough. Chill the dough.

Roll out to about 1/8-inch thickness; cut into circles. Place the circles on a buttered cookie sheet and prick the top of each with a fork. Bake in a moderate oven (350 degrees) about 8 minutes. Makes 80, 1 1/2-inch cookies.

Note: When testing this recipe, I used 2 1/2 to 3 cups flour, plus a bit more for rolling out the dough.

I thought they would be better topped with a light icing. I iced some of them and sprinkled colored sugar on the rest. I thought it improved them—and I hope Martha would agree.

Sugar Caster

John and Abigail Pudding

Chapter 9

Sweet Treats

Children have enlivened presidential Christmas celebrations since the year 1800, when John and Abigail Adams organized a party in a frigid White House. Because the numerous fireplaces just couldn't keep the drafty old mansion warm, the entire house was cold, damp and unfinished. Abigail complained, "Not a single room is finished of a whole."

To make the place bearable for their first Christmas and in an attempt to dry the plaster on the wall, she burned 20 cords of wood in each of the fireplaces. Before the children's party, members of Congress and their wives arrived for a reception. One account reports that the first lady was "distressed and embarrassed because it was still cold." Guests left early.

The children's party that followed seemed warmer because of its uninhibited joviality. Susanna, the president's grandchild, was the only child resident at the new executive mansion. (It was not called the "White House" until Teddy Roosevelt's administration. It was, in fact, brownish in color. After the burning by the British in 1814, it was painted white.)

Susanna had received from Santa a beautiful set of dishes for her dolls, but an envious playmate at the Christmas Day party smashed them. In retaliation, Susanna bit the nose and cheeks off her playmate's new wax doll. Pandemonium broke out, and President Adams himself had to quiet the guests and soothe injured feelings. Mrs. Adams came to the rescue by serving all the guests her wonderful Christmas Plum Pudding.

Christmas Plum Pudding

2 pounds raisins

1 pound golden raisins

1 pound currants

4 cups bread crumbs

1 quart beef suet, chopped fine

1 cup citron, cut fine

4 tablespoons candied orange peel, cut fine

4 tablespoons candied lemon peel, cut fine

2 teaspoons nutmeg

1 teaspoon salt

1 teaspoon ginger

12 eggs, beaten

1 cup brandy

Milk, as needed

Hard Sauce

In a large mixing bowl, combine raisins, currants, bread crumbs, suet, citron, orange peel, lemon peel, nutmeg, salt and ginger. Beat eggs; stir into mixture. Add brandy and, if not

Plum Pudding

John and Abigail Pudding (cont.)

Chapter 9

Sweet Treats

moist enough, add milk to make mixture cling together. Spoon into closed pudding forms with tight-fitting lids. Place in boiling water; boil gently for 4 to 5 hours. Water must be boiling when the pudding is put in. As the water evaporates away, add more boiling water. Keep forms covered. Before turning out, plunge into cold water (for a minute). Serve with Hard Sauce. Decorate each pudding with a sprig of holly.

Hard Sauce

    1/3 cup butter

    1 cup sugar (powdered, brown or maple)

    1 teaspoon flavoring (vanilla, rum or
       sherry)

Cream butter until soft. Stir in sugar and flavoring. Cool until ready to use.

Plum Pudding

Teddy's Clove Cake

9

Chapter

Sweet Treats

When Theodore Roosevelt lived in the White House, he followed a dedicated regimen. The dinner hour for small meals was set at half past 7. For banquets, the time was pushed back to 8 p.m.

There was hardly a night without guests, so dinner was served in the state dining room. The private dining room was used only for family meals such as breakfast, luncheons and a few dinners. If any guests were invited for one of these meals, it was only for friends of the six children and the governess.

White House banquets of the period speak of fine linens, elaborate flowers, beautiful crystal, fine china, and silver or gilt tableware. The dinners were usually from eight to 12 courses, and the entire meal was served in two hours. The steward reported that only the choicest sections of a roast leg of lamb or fillet of beef were served. One leg or one fillet would feed four or five persons. Three French chefs were employed to prepare these state banquets.

The usual kitchen staff consisted of a cook and several helpers who prepared the food for the family dining room. One of the popular and favorite desserts for the family was a Clove Cake.

Clove Cake

2 eggs

1 stick (1/2 cup) butter, softened

1/2 cup milk

1 teaspoon soda

1/2 cup molasses

2 cups flour

1/2 teaspoon cloves

1/2 teaspoon cinnamon

1 1/2 teaspoons nutmeg

3 cups raisins

1/2 pound crystallized ginger and melted butter, for decoration

In a bowl, mix the eggs, butter and milk; beat well. Add the soda to molasses and combine with egg mixture. In another bowl, mix flour with cloves, cinnamon and nutmeg. Gradually add the egg mixture to the flour mixture; beat well. Fold in raisins. Grease an 8-inch tube pan; add batter. Bake at 350 degrees for 45 to 55 minutes. Turn onto a rack to cool, brush the top with some melted butter, and garnish with overlapping slices of crystallized ginger.

Flour

CHRISTMAS IN THE CAPITOL

CHAPTER 9

Sweet Treats

Eighteenth-century Virginians took their holiday celebrations seriously. George Washington, for example, always kept Christmas with an abundance of joy and merrymaking. Their English heritage and Anglican faith had much to do with their bright view of the season. The period of lusty eating, drinking, entertaining and good fellowship that had characterized Christmas in the halls of feudal England had much in common with that in Tidewater, Va.

Merrymaking was a strenuous activity, the festivities lasting for more than a month. The traditional European boar's head and peacock of Christmas had given way to the turkey and venison of the Virginia plantations.

The feasting and merriment kept its lusty quality. During the day, the men pitched quits, rode to the hounds, hunted, raced or fought their gamecocks, with occasional spells of quiet for courting, politics or business matters. By night, there was much feasting, singing, dancing, and carousing, and gaming, with more and more intensified courting. Such diversions as cards, dice, backgammon and chess were available for those who fancied them, while "Blind-Man's Bluff," "Hoop and Hide," "Hunt the Slipper," and other games of chance involving much random kissing and laughter were favorites with men and women alike.

Washington and Jefferson both tried to be "home for Christmas." Washington returned to his beloved Mount Vernon on Christmas Eve to greet his family, friends and servants, where there were rousing cheers, songs, pistol shots and firecrackers, followed by a great feast.

The first record of a grand Christmas party in the White House was given by Dolley Madison in 1811. The coveted invitations to guests read simply: "President Madison and I would be greatly honored to have you dine with us on Christmas evening."

Entertaining was quite inexpensive at that time. Turkeys cost 75 cents each, ducks 50 cents, and a whole suckling pig only $3. Waiters, generally slaves, were rented for the party and paid 35 cents each.

The one dish that seems to be included in these early Christmas parties was Wine Jelly Mold. All of the early presidents from Virginia served it, the recipe perhaps being passed along by the various first ladies or their chefs. In recent times, Rosalynn Carter served it at the White House and for Christmas "at home" in Plains, Ga.

The original recipe called for four calves feet without taking off the hooves. The modern recipe uses unflavored gelatin.

Wine

9

CHAPTER

Sweet Treats

WINE JELLY MOLD

2 envelopes unflavored gelatin

1/2 cup cold water

2 cups strained juice (grape,
  cranberry or raspberry), heated to boiling

3/4 to 1 cup sugar

Pinch of salt

1 pint red wine (Madeira, sherry or
  Burgundy)

Juice of 3 lemons

Fresh fruit for garnish

Dissolve the gelatin in the cold water and add to the boiling fruit juice. Add sugar to taste with a pinch of salt.

Let cool. Add the wine and lemon juice. Pour into a fancy ring mold that has been chilled. Refrigerate for at least 2 hours or until well set. Unmold on a cold platter and decorate with pieces of fresh fruits that have been rolled in confectioners' sugar.

Wine

Pineapple Upside-Down Cake

Chapter 9

Sweet Treats

Pineapples were discovered by some of Columbus' men on the West Indian Island of Guadeloupe during his second voyage in 1493. Its flavor and fragrance astonished and delighted them.

In 1519, Magellan's ships stopped in Brazil to pick up sweet pineapples for the crews. In 1595, Sir Walter Raleigh reported on the great abundance of pina, the princess of fruits. The Portuguese are given credit for shipping it to India in 1556, during the reign of the Mogul emperor Akbar. The fruit did not appear on any of the Pacific islands until Captain Cook went about planting them in 1777.

Americans knew of the existence of pineapple in 1751 when George Washington visited the warm island of Barbados and confided to his diary that of all the unknown fruits he had tasted there, "None please my taste as does the pine."

Americans today eat mostly Hawaiian and Puerto Rican pineapples. Even though Hawaii dominates the world market, the fruit was not cultivated there on any grand scale until the 1880s. It was not until this century that Hawaii became the leading producer of pineapple. Peak production came in 1951. At this time, some large producers began to move parts of their operations elsewhere—to the Philippines, where labor was cheaper, and to Kenya and Thailand. Hawaii remains the largest pineapple producer, but its share of the world market has been diminished.

Pineapples are generally available year-round but are best in April and May. When buying the fruit, look for bright green leaves and a firm skin. Smell the base: if it has a pleasing pineapple aroma, chances are it will prove flavorful. Pineapples should be refrigerated until used.

An updated version of an American classic is this Fresh Pineapple Upside-Down Cake, made with fresh pineapple instead of the usual canned. A whole pineapple will not be needed for the cake, so the excess may be used in a salad or just eaten fresh.

Fresh Pineapple Upside-Down Cake

1 small ripe pineapple
6 tablespoons butter
1 cup dark brown sugar, packed
Maraschino cherries
1 stick (1/2 cup) butter
1 cup granulated sugar

2 eggs
1 teaspoon lemon zest
1 teaspoon orange zest
1 3/4 cups flour
2 teaspoons baking powder
1/4 teaspoon cinnamon
Grated nutmeg
Pinch of salt

Pine Apple

PINEAPPLE UPSIDE-DOWN CAKE (CONT.)

CHAPTER

9

*Sweet
Treats*

1/2 cup buttermilk
2 tablespoons dark rum

Peel the pineapple and slice it into 1/2-inch circles. Remove core. Melt the 6 tablespoons butter in a 10-inch frying pan. Swirl to coat the bottom. Sprinkle the brown sugar evenly over the butter. Arrange pineapple slices on the bottom of the pan. If you are a purist, arrange cherries decoratively.

Prepare the batter by creaming 1 stick (1/2 cup) butter and granulated sugar. Add eggs, one at a time, and continue beating for 2 or 3 minutes. Stir in lemon and orange zest. Sift the flour with baking powder, salt, cinnamon and nutmeg. Add dry ingredients to the egg mixture in three batches, alternating with the buttermilk. Stir in rum and gently pour over the pineapple. Bake in a 350- degree oven for 45 minutes. Test for doneness. Cool on a rack before inverting on a plate. May be served plain or with a dab of sweetened whipped cream.

Pine Apple

MERINGUES

CHAPTER 9

Sweet Treats

Meringues are one of the most versatile of desserts. They are light, airy and provide the basis for clever desserts. Almost as important, they are inexpensive, elegant and not even particularly fattening, as the sugar added for each serving is minimal. Even broken pieces can be added in rich ice cream and puddings.

For successful meringues, it is essential to separate the eggs carefully and to use a perfectly clean, dry bowl when beating the whites. A copper bowl is ideal, but stainless steel may be used. The extra volume you will get in using a copper bowl is about one egg. With the saving of one egg per recipe, over the years of whipping egg whites you should be able to afford such a bowl.

Store any leftover yolks covered with water in a sealed container in the refrigerator for two or three days for later use. Meringues can be kept crisp for two weeks in an airtight container. Small meringues will keep for four to six months, if frozen. Large meringues do not freeze as well, picking up moisture and losing crispness.

A popular meringue from Australia made with apples is crisp on the outside and soft within. This elegant tart can be quickly assembled by using a ready-made pastry shell, if you so desire.

APPLE MERINGUE TART

2 pounds cooking apples, peeled, and
   chopped
1 tablespoon water
2 tablespoons butter
8 tablespoons sugar
5 tablespoons apricot jam
1/2 teaspoon cinnamon
1 baked pastry shell, 8 to 9 inches
Meringue Topping

Cook apples in saucepan with water and butter until soft; add sugar and stir well. Puree apples; return to saucepan. Add apricot jam, cinnamon and stir over moderate heat until liquid has been evaporated. Pour this thick puree into a pastry shell; smooth top.

MERINGUE TOPPING

2 egg whites
Pinch of salt
8 tablespoons sugar
2 teaspoons cornstarch
1/8 teaspoon vanilla
1 teaspoon malt vinegar
2 tablespoons split, blanched almonds

To make Meringue Topping, whip whites with salt until stiff. Mix sugar and cornstarch; whisk into whites a spoonful at a time, whisking after each addition. Add vanilla and vinegar; whisk again. Pile meringue on top to cover surface, using a spoon to make soft peaks all over the top. Stand almonds upright, spaced evenly. Bake for one hour at 275 degrees. Serve warm or cold.

Tart Pan

The Awesome Apple

Chapter 9

Sweet Treats

Apples capture the essence of fall colors. Their glowing crimsons, lemony yellows, splashed pinks and greens are all part of the season. They vary in flavor from tart with a sweet aftertaste to spicy. Some are mild and subtle; others burst with flavor. Without question, the apple is the king of fruits.

Reference books tell us that apples originated in southeastern Europe and southwestern Asia. It was the Romans who introduced them to northern Europe. Carbonized apples have been found in Anatolia dated at 6500 B.C. Ramses II had them planted in Egypt in the 13th century B.C., but the fruit was rare and expensive. An early solon decreed that at a marriage the bridal couple might eat only one apple between them before going to bed.

The apple with the longest history is the Api, named for the Etruscan horticulturist who developed it. It has remained in high esteem through the centuries. Louis XIII had the api grown in his gardens at Orleans in 1628, deeming it the only one worthy to be served to Louis XV. It can still be bought in France under its original name, the pomme d Api. In the United States, it is possible to find it under the name "Lady Apple." In colonial days, it was held in high esteem and sought at Christmas as a special treat.

From the beginning, the apple has played a part in religion, magic, superstition, folklore, history and medicine, but it did not figure in the first example likely to pop into your mind—the story of Adam and Eve. You could probably win a bet by wagering there is no mention of the apple in Genesis. It is cited in other parts of the Bible, but not in connection with Adam and Eve. What they ate was "the fruit of the tree of knowledge of good and evil," otherwise unidentified.

The spread of apple territory has been dramatized by the folk hero known as Johnny Appleseed, whose name was John Chapman, born in 1774 in Leominster, Mass. He did not prowl the countryside scattering seeds at random, knowing that apples do not grow true from seeds. Instead, he established nurseries for apple seedlings. He owned nurseries in western Pennsylvania in 1800, and by 1845 he had established a chain of nurseries from the Allegheny River to Ohio, and as far west as Indiana, where he died at Fort Wayne.

Today, the state of Washington produces up to 35 million bushels of apples per year. When combined with other apple production throughout the country, America is the top producer in the world with an estimated 100 million bushels annually.

Apple

THE AWESOME APPLE (CONT.)

CHAPTER 9

Sweet Treats

The selection of apples in markets today is extensive. There are three basic types—eating, all-purpose, and cooking. Red Delicious is the sweetest eating apple; the Golden Delicious is an all-purpose apple, tart, sweet, juicy and full-flavored; Staymans and Granny Smiths are good for pies; Jonathans are fabulous in salads; and Rome Beauties and York Imperials are ideal for baking. With the big selection available today, there is an apple for use in hundreds of ways.

Everyone has a favorite pie or cobbler recipe. This recipe for an apple cake is one I'm sure you will enjoy. It keeps and carries well so it is a great picnic pleaser. For that matter, I like it best when it is a day old.

APPLE CAKE

4 cups sliced apples

2 eggs

2 cups sugar

1 cup golden raisins

1 cup walnuts, chopped

1/4 teaspoon cinnamon

1/2 cup oil

2 teaspoons vanilla extract

2 teaspoons baking soda

2 cups sugar

2 cups flour

3/4 teaspoon salt

In a large bowl, break the eggs over the apples and toss with a fork. Add the sugar, raisins, nuts, cinnamon, oil and vanilla. Sift the dry ingredients together and add to the apple-egg mixture. Mix well. Spread the batter into a greased and floured 9x12-inch pan. Bake at 350 degrees for 45 minutes. When cool, sprinkle with powdered sugar. Cut into squares to serve.

Apple

PUMPKIN CHEESECAKE

CHAPTER 9

Sweet Treats

Pumpkins are native to America. In 1540, Spanish explorer Coronado reported that the natives of the Southwest grew them and ate them with most of their meals. Later when Cartier explored the St. Lawrence region, he found pumpkins growing throughout the region and referred to them as "big melons." When the English settled in Virginia, the pumpkin was already growing and quickly became their most available vegetable. The Indians in New England taught the first Pilgrims how to use the gourds as a food, which may have been responsible for their survival.

We all know that Cinderella rode to the king's ball in a pumpkin coach drawn by field mice. David Thoreau stated that he would rather sit on a pumpkin he had all to himself than be crowded on a velvet cushion. Today, we know it is most often used as a filling for pumpkin pie and has become a tradition for Thanksgiving feasts. Early American cookbooks listed recipes for pumpkin butter, pumpkin pickles, pumpkin french fries and even pumpkin beer. In other parts of the world, pumpkins are simmered in soups, baked with meats and served with ravioli or pasta.

This recipe for Pumpkin Cheesecake could become a new favorite—and a welcome change from the traditional pumpkin pie.

PUMPKIN CHEESECAKE CRUST

1 1/2 cups (8 ounces) cinnamon- flavored
    graham crackers or
  gingersnap crumbs
1 stick (1/2 cup) butter, melted

Crush cookies to fine crumbs. Mix in melted butter, blending thoroughly. Press mixture into the bottom and along the sides of a 10-inch springform pan; chill 20 minutes. Heat oven to 325 degrees.

FILLING

24 ounces cream cheese, room
    temperature
1 1/4 cups sugar
5 eggs
2 cups pumpkin puree
3 tablespoons rum
2 teaspoons vanilla extract
1 teaspoon cinnamon
1/2 teaspoon ginger
1/4 teaspoon nutmeg
1/8 teaspoon cloves
1/8 teaspoon cardamom
1/8 teaspoon allspice

Pumpkin

PUMPKIN CHEESECAKE (CONT.)

CHAPTER 9

Sweet Treats

In a mixing bowl, beat cream cheese and sugar until smooth. Beat in the eggs, one at a time, until the mixture is light and fluffy. In another bowl, combine pumpkin with the rum, vanilla and spices. Beat until smooth. Beat the pumpkin mixture into the cream cheese mixture. Pour this combined filling into the crust and bake for 1 1/4 hours or until set.

TOPPING

2 cups dairy sour cream
1/3 cup sugar
2 tablespoons rum

Whisk the sour cream, sugar and rum until smooth. Spoon the mixture on top of the cheesecake. Turn off the oven and let the cake cool in the oven. (This will prevent the top from cracking.) When cool, refrigerate for at least 6 hours before serving. Serves 10 to 12.

Pumpkin

Pork Cake? Yes—Pork Cake!

Chapter 9

Sweet Treats

From early colonial times, native sons of both Virginia and New England have had a running argument as to where the first American cookbook was published.

I have no accurate information on when the first New England cookbook was issued, but I do know that the "Williamsburg Cook Book" was published in Williamsburg, Va., in 1742. The original volume was written in Old English, with Old English spellings as well as instructions, often calling for a "pinch of this" and a "handful of that." The following recipe for Virginia Pork Cake incorporates modern measurements and instructions.

Virginia Pork Cake

2 teaspoons soda

2 cups boiling water

3 cups sugar

3 eggs, beaten

1 pound fat salt pork

1 1/2 cups walnuts

1/4 pound citron

1 teaspoon vanilla extract (rum extract may be used)

3 1/2 cups flour

1 teaspoon cinnamon

1 teaspoon ground cloves

1 teaspoon nutmeg

1 pound raisins

1 pound currants

Dissolve soda in boiling water. Stir in sugar; beat until sugar is dissolved. Add beaten eggs; stir until well mixed.

Grind together the salt pork, walnuts and citron; add to sugar mixture with vanilla or rum. Sift flour with cinnamon, cloves and nutmeg; mix into batter with raisins and currants.

Pour batter into three buttered and lightly floured loaf pans. Bake at 350 degrees for 15 minutes. Reduce heat to 325 degrees and continue to bake for one hour.

Remove from oven; cool on racks. When cool, wrap each loaf in cheese-cloth that has been moistened with a good make of spirits. (These instructions are directly from the cookbook. I assume they mean with rum or brandy.)

The Virginia colonists, as a rule, ate well and either imported the ingredients they needed or grew them. This cake is a heavy cake and not too sweet. I would suggest serving it with a hot or cold sauce of your choice.

Nuts

Moravian Cookies

The early Moravian settlers of Pennsylvania and North Carolina brought with them an old custom of the love feast, a traditional feast originating with the early Christians in commemoration of the Last Supper. In North Carolina, the feast was expanded and celebrated at least five times a year.

One of these five times was at Christmas, when the feast is intended to rekindle a spirit of love. The original feast was given at church to the accompaniment of choral singing. Depending upon the season, either sweet feast buns, sugar cake or Christmas cookies were served with a cup of coffee made by brewing coffee with milk and sugar. The celebration has now moved to homes, where several types of buns, biscuits and sugar cakes are served. For the Christmas feast, Christmas cookies are served with coffee, tea or cider if in season.

Moravian Christmas Cookies

1/2 cup brown sugar, firmly packed

3/4 teaspoon baking soda

1/2 teaspoon salt

3/4 teaspoon ginger

3/4 teaspoon cloves

1/4 teaspoon nutmeg

3/4 teaspoon cinnamon

1/4 teaspoon allspice

1 cup molasses

1 stick (1/2 cup) butter

4 cups flour

Sift together the brown sugar, baking soda, salt, ginger, cloves, nutmeg, cinnamon and allspice. Heat the molasses to boiling point, but don't boil. Stir in butter until smooth. Cool slightly then pour into a large mixing bowl; beat in sugar-spice mixture. Hand knead in flour until the dough holds its shape. Form into a ball; chill in refrigerator until firm. The dough will keep for weeks if wrapped. Break off pieces of dough; roll until paper thin on a lightly floured surface. Cut into rounds or into any Christmas cookie shapes. Place on a greased cookie sheet and bake at 375 degrees for 6 to 8 minutes. Makes 8 dozen cookies.

Ladle & Spoon

COOKING WITH APPLES

9

CHAPTER

*Sweet
Treats*

If your house is like mine, I'm sure you get pretty tired of all the rich, heavy foods of the Christmas/New Year season.

Now is the time to use some of the supplies of fresh fruits you have bought or been given.

Apples and pears are abundant in the markets, if you were not lucky enough to receive them as gifts. Apples have always been at the top of the list for tasty and simple dishes. Through the years they have been prepared for desserts in hundreds of ways as well as for side dishes and salads.

I received as a gift some individual apple bakers. They are about 6 inches in diameter and have a spike in the center to slip the cored apple over for baking. They were made in England, are oven-proof, most attractive, and came from a local shop.

HONEY-BAKED APPLES

6 large baking apples
3 tablespoons chopped pecans
3 tablespoons raisins
1 cup water
1/3 cup honey
1 stick (2 inches long) cinnamon
1 tablespoon lemon juice

Core apples; peel the top third of each one. Place in a shallow baking pan or individual bakers (as mentioned above). Combine pecans and raisins; stuff cavities of apples with nut mixture.

Combine honey, water and cinnamon in saucepan; bring to a boil. Reduce heat; simmer five minutes. Remove from heat; stir in lemon juice.

Remove cinnamon stick from liquid; pour over apples. Cover and bake at 350 degrees for 45 to 50 minutes, or until the apples are tender. Remove cover and let apples brown a bit if they are not already browned. Baste at least once during baking.

A great American apple dish, served as a side dish for breakfast, is Fried Apples with Bacon. This delicious dish is easy and quick to prepare.

FRIED APPLES WITH BACON

4 tart apples
1/2 pound bacon
3 tablespoons sugar

Peel apples, and cut into cubes. Fry bacon until crisp and drain on paper towel; keep warm.

Drain all but about 1/4 cup of the bacon fat from skillet. Add apple cubes to fill the skillet; sprinkle with sugar. Cover and cook slowly until apples are tender. Remove cover and gently turn apples. Cook until lightly browned. Serve on a hot platter with the bacon and scrambled eggs. Serves at least 6.

Honey

THE REFRESHING MELON

9

CHAPTER

Sweet Treats

Melons are refreshing, light, sweet and juicy, and have been around for hundreds of years. New varieties are being introduced every year. It is believed that melons originally came from Asia, spread to France via Italy, and later to Africa and then to Spain before being introduced to America. They are now cultivated in any hot sunny area of the world.

Melons are made up of about 94 percent water and contain both vitamins A and C. They have fewer calories than many other popular fruits.

In checking the markets I was surprised to find all of the old favorites plus several interesting newcomers. Of course, the watermelon is most popular and is available in a familiar red-meated variety that is supposed to be seedless—and a yellow-meated one. The latter is becoming more popular and will soon be readily available. Watermelons are a distinct genus.

The other melons I discovered fall into three main groups: cantaloupes, which have the most fragrant flesh; "netted" or muskmelons, which have a raised pattern on the outside skin and a scented flesh; and the oval or round winter melons. Some of these will be common and some are new and more exotic. The ones most of us know are the cantaloupe, crenshaw, Persian and casaba. Some of the lesser-known melons are the Juan canary, a Santa Claus or Christmas melon, a Sharly and a new orange honeydew. All of these I found available in local markets.

Melon is usually served raw as a breakfast fruit or as an hors d'oeuvre or dessert. A chilled melon may be served in slices, wedges, balls or individual cups and garnished with fresh mint or drizzled with a liqueur or sweet wine. The scooped-out shells made into cups or baskets make a dazzling presentation. Next time try a sprinkle of ground ginger on your cantaloupe.

A refreshing summer season melon dessert is this Melon Lime Mousse.

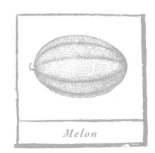

Melon

The Refreshing Melon (cont.)

Chapter 9

Sweet Treats

Melon Lime Mousse

1/2 honeydew melon, medium size, very
    ripe (about 1 1/2 pounds)
1/8 teaspoon ground ginger
1 lime, zest (grated rind) and juice
2 tablespoons plain yogurt
1/4 cup sugar
2 eggs, separated
1 tablespoon unflavored gelatin

Scoop out melon flesh; drain in colander.
Puree in a blender or food processor. Turn the
puree into a bowl; add ginger, lime zest, yogurt
and all but 1 1/2 teaspoons lime juice. Mix
well; set aside.

Whisk egg yolks and sugar in a bowl over
a pan of hot water until pale in color and
slightly thickened. Remove from heat. Pour
melon puree into egg mixture and stir until

well blended. Dissolve gelatin in 2 tablespoons
water; melt over hot water. Remove from heat;
cool.

Add gelatin to melon mixture and stir well
to dissolve gelatin. Cover and leave in a cool
place until slightly thickened to a syrupy
consistency but not set. Whip egg whites until
stiff; fold into melon mixture. Pour into serving
bowl; chill about two hours or until set.
Garnish with slices of lime. The mousse also
may be garnished with kiwi fruit that has been
sprinkled with remaining lime juice.
Serves 6 to 8.

Melon

John Tyler's Transparent Pudding

When John Tyler assumed the reins of the presidency after the sudden death of William Henry Harrison, at his side was his wife, Letitia Christian Tyler. Both were unceremonious, hospitable Virginians, who brought their Virginia way of life to the mansion. They extended a warm, spontaneous welcome to all who came to call.

Their dinners and receptions were characterized by a warmth and graciousness inherent to a son and daughter of the Old Dominion. For two years after his wife's death, President Tyler lived simply and comfortably at the White House. Then, in the winter of 1843, he met Julia Gardiner, a high-spirited young girl with a highly developed sense of superiority and grandeur.

Julia was the daughter of David Gardiner of Gardiner's Island, N.Y. When she arrived in the nation's capital, she was an internationally known beauty, fresh from triumphs in the most select circles of London, Paris, Rome and New York. Most every man who met her fell under her spell. The resident of the White House was no exception. Within months after their first meeting, Tyler asked her to marry him. He was 53; she 23.

The difference in their ages did not suit this beautiful, fun-loving lady, and so the matter was dropped. Then in the early spring of 1844, while on a presidential cruise, one of the ship's guns exploded causing the death of Julia's father. After a state funeral in the East Room of the White House, President Tyler spent a great deal of time with the grief-stricken daughter. Their rapport slowly grew. The age difference seemed less important. Within three months, Julia Gardiner became the second Mrs. John Tyler.

With only eight months left in Tyler's term of office, Julia decided to make the most of it. Accustomed to the high society of Europe, she set about to duplicate it, receiving her guests in regal splendor, seated in a large armchair on a slightly raised platform, 12 maids surrounding her. Julia was very much a queen, from the crown of three enormous curled feathers that adorned her head to the purple velvet gown with a long train. Each guest was announced as he entered the room.

Julia was determined to leave the White House in a blaze of glory. She planned a grand ball and sent out 2,000 invitations for February 1845. A gala occasion with enormous bouquets of flowers and side tables loaded with every imaginable delicacy, all political feuds were forgotten as every senator and representative rushed to pay their respects to the beautiful first lady. The event was lauded in Washington for years

Apricots

John Tyler's Transparent Pudding (cont.)

9
Chapter
Sweet Treats

to come. President Tyler, a lame duck in the presidency, joked, "They cannot now say I am a president without a party."

Julia flatly stated that "Everyone adores me," and it was probably inconceivable to the lovely woman that someone might not. Her husband was so infatuated that he agreed.

Today, we would worry about the calories in the rich dishes and desserts she had served, but it is unlikely the self-assured Julia ever gave calories a second thought. We are certain she ate and enjoyed a goodly share of rich puddings in her lifetime. This recipe for Transparent Pudding was one of her favorites.

Transparent Pudding

2 cups dried apricots, figs, and dates,
    mixed together
1 cup sugar
2 sticks (1 cup) butter
8 egg yolks
Whipped heavy cream

In a saucepan, stew the dried fruit in water to cover, until tender. Remove from the heat; drain. Butter a large baking dish and cover the bottom with fruit. Cream the sugar and butter. Beat the egg yolks and add to creamed mixture. Pour over the fruit and bake in a slow oven at 300 to 325 degrees for 30 minutes. Remove from the oven and, when cool, turn out on a large platter. Refrigerate. Just before serving, garnish with sweetened whipped cream and maraschino cherries. Makes 6 to 8 servings.

Apricots

Chester Arthur, Gourmet

If "gourmetship" were important in ranking presidents, then Chester Arthur would be at the top of the list—or second only to Thomas Jefferson.

When Arthur became president after the death of Garfield, he refused to move into the White House unless it was remodeled feeling it to be a poorly kept barracks. He informed Congress that if they did not appropriate the funds then he would pay for it himself. He was lucky that he did not have to pay for the changes, for the repairs were considerable.

He hired Louis Tiffany of New York to undertake the innovations in decor. He supervised the progress daily, but the room he gave the most attention to was the private dining room. The elegance of the room was almost overwhelming. The wallpaper was of heavy gold paper with draperies of pomegranate plush set off by wall lights of crimson glass.

Arthur was fastidious in his clothing, his food, wine, sense of decor and style. His wife Ellen had died prior to his becoming president. Thus, his younger sister Mary, wife of the Rev. John E. McElroy, assisted him with his official entertaining. His son was away at school most of the time. His 10-year-old daughter lived at the White House but was shielded from the spotlight.

Arthur insisted on the finest and wanted it served in the best manner. White House fare was a model of the finest cuisine of the day. His dinners were vastly elegant. The flowers, the linens, the silver, the attendants, all showed the latest style with complete abandon in expense and taste.

During the social and holiday seasons, a Nesselrode Pudding was popular and added to this elegant era. The dessert is similar to Charlotte Russe.

Nesselrode Pudding

2 tablespoons unflavored gelatin

3 cups milk

2/3 cup sugar

5 eggs, separated

2/3 cup chopped raisins

3 tablespoons ground almonds

1/4 pound broken macaroons

1 1/2 tablespoons rum or brandy

2 teaspoons vanilla

1/8 teaspoon salt

Maraschino cherries for garnish

Whipped heavy cream

Cherries

CHESTER ARTHUR, GOURMET (CONT.)

CHAPTER 9

Sweet Treats

Dissolve gelatin in 1 cup milk. Heat 2 cups milk in top of double boiler; add sugar and stir to dissolve. Add egg yolks, slightly beaten, and cook, stirring constantly until slightly thickened. Stir in dissolved gelatin. Add raisins, almonds and crumbled macaroons. Mix well; remove from heat. Cool slightly and add rum or brandy and vanilla; let cool.

Beat egg whites until stiff, adding the salt as you beat. Fold whites into cooled mixture. Pour into a wet, fancy pudding mold; chill several hours. At serving time, unmold the pudding on an elegant silver tray and garnish with maraschino cherries. Pass whipped cream separately. Cream may be sweetened and flavored, if you choose. Makes 12 servings.

Cherries

A Viennese Dessert

CHAPTER 9

Sweet Treats

Every great dessert, in order to gain stature, has either a reason or a story to its birth. The Hungarian and Austrian societies challenged all others in the invention of great pastries. Two classic Hungarian pastries are known as the Dobos Torte and the Indianer.

In 1813, it was fashionable for the Hungarian aristocracy to live most of the time in Vienna and there pursue some private hobby. So it was during that year that Count Ferdinand Palffy purchased the Theater an der Wein so that he could play the game of international producer. The theater was not a success. He tried to spice up the acts with jugglers.

One of the acts was an East Indian magician, but Vienna did not react to this showmanship. In desperation, Count Palffy, who also was a well-known gourmet of the time, asked his Hungarian pastry chef to bake an unusual dessert to be handed out during intermission to remind those in the audience of the Indian in the show.

The resulting dessert was a fist-sized doughnut that was baked and then hollowed out, filled with whipped cream and topped with chocolate. This shining dark brown sweet created an immediate sensation. And indeed, the next day everyone was enraptured—not with the play, but with the new black and white cake. Within a week, every pastry shop had lines of patrons demanding the new cake, and shops soon stopped making their other pastries because no one would buy anything but Indianer. Though the chef is unknown, the name of the cake is retained to this day.

Indianer

4 eggs, separated

Pinch of salt

2/3 cup granulated sugar

2/3 cup flour

1/4 pound sweet chocolate

1 tablespoon unsalted butter

1 cup heavy cream

3 tablespoons vanilla sugar (or granulated sugar)

Heat the oven to 250 degrees. Whip the egg whites with a pinch of salt until they are foamy and stand in peaks. Add egg yolks, one at a time, beating for 2 minutes after each addition. Add the sugar gradually; whip for 2 minutes. Then add flour, a little at a time, stirring until smooth.

Butter a special Indianer form, if you have one (a muffin tin or individual Bundt pans may be substituted). Fill 12 forms about three-fourths full with batter. Bake for 10 to 12 minutes.

Milk Maid

A Viennese Dessert (cont.)

Chapter 9

Sweet Treats

When the cakes are cool, cut across into halves and scrape out the center of each half. Make the glaze by placing chocolate in the top of a double boiler; soften over hot water while stirring. Let chocolate cool a bit; whip in butter. Dip the top half in the chocolate and chill in refrigerator. Whip cream until stiff, sweetening with 3 tablespoons vanilla sugar or granulated sugar with a teaspoon of vanilla extract. Fill the hollowed halves with whipped cream. Place chocolate-glazed tops on the filled halves. The whipped cream should show around the middle, resembling grinning teeth. (These may resemble a rich cupcake in America. In Hungary or Austria, they are considered French pastry.)

Milk Maid

SWEDISH GINGERSNAPS

CHAPTER 9

Sweet Treats

In Sweden, the best-loved food festivals of the year begin with the "Festival of Light," Santa Lucia Day, Dec. 13, which celebrates the gradual return of more hours of daylight to the dark Swedish winter. This festival is followed by Advent and Christmas.

The role of Santa Lucia is played by a daughter in a household and is sometimes aided by an honor guard made up of other little girls. She rises early in the morning and puts on a long white dress. Wearing a crown of lingonberry leaves studded with candles, she comes to her parents' bedroom bearing trays of fresh saffron yeast buns, coffee and special Lucia gingersnap biscuits called pepparkakor. Sometimes a more spirited beverage such as Glogg is included in her festive fare.

This traditional gingersnap recipe takes a little time to make and can be started the night before Lucia.

PEPPARKAKOR (SWEDISH GINGERSNAPS)

6 tablespoons butter

1/2 cup sugar

2 tablespoons golden syrup

4 tablespoons water

1 teaspoon soda

1 cup plus 1 tablespoon flour

1 1/4 teaspoons cinnamon

1 teaspoon powdered ginger

In a saucepan, combine the butter, sugar, syrup and water; heat over medium heat. Stir until the butter melts and remove from heat; stir until cooled. Mix soda, flour, cinnamon and ginger. Stir in cooled butter mixture and knead together. Leave dough to rest for at least 4 hours or overnight in a cool (not cold) place, covered with plastic wrap so it does not dry out.

Heat oven to 425 degrees. Grease several cookie sheets. Lightly flour a working surface and a rolling pin. Roll out dough a small piece at a time to avoid mixing in too much extra flour. Roll very thin; cut into heart shapes or small rounds with a cookie cutter. Place on greased cookie sheets and bake at 425 degrees for 5 to 7 minutes. Move to a wire rack while hot; cool. When cold, store in an airtight container. This recipe makes from 80 to 100 snaps.

Coffee Pot

Jefferson Hospitality

Thomas Jefferson was the greatest connoisseur of fine food and wine to live in the White House.

After he was inaugurated, Jefferson took his time moving in, finally occupying the residence on March 19, since it took that long to bring from Monticello his furniture, servants, decorative accessories and scientific collections. He brought servants familiar with his mode of life, his hospitality and generosity. Consequently the rooms immediately took on an intimate, friendly atmosphere.

Within a few weeks after he moved in, he abolished the weekly levee and issued a declaration that each year he would hold two large receptions—one on New Year's Day and the other on the Fourth of July, to which all were welcome. This was appropriate since we would not enjoy such a celebration if he had not written the Declaration of Independence in 1776.

When he needed a hostess, Jefferson called on Dolley Madison, wife of his Secretary of State. She presided at his table and helped take care of his guests. Even though he chose to limit the formality of his entertaining, there was never a limit to his hospitality.

His invitations often were worded: "Th. Jefferson requests the favor of Mr. and Mrs. Smith to dine with him on Tuesday next at half after three, and any friends who may be with them."

At the Fourth of July celebration, Jefferson shook hands with all his guests. Refreshments were served to all comers and the excellent Marine Corps band played martial music. Fresh-made ice cream was essential, Mrs. Madison providing the recipe. Both vanilla and pink peppermint flavors were served. Dolley Madison's recipe for Pink Peppermint Ice Cream would be just as fitting and mouth-watering for your own celebration.

Pink Peppermint Ice Cream

1 pound peppermint-stick candy
1 quart light cream
1 quart heavy cream, whipped
Sugar to taste

Crush peppermint-stick candy and soak in the 1 quart light cream. Allow to stand until dissolved. Add 1 quart heavy cream, whipped. Sweeten with sugar to taste. Pour into an ice cream freezer and pack the tub with chopped ice and 4 handfuls salt. Turn until stiff and frozen. Pack with more ice to let it set up until ready to serve.

A Bachelor President

Chapter 9

Sweet Treats

The citizens of the United States elected James Buchanan, our only unmarried president, in 1856.

With President Buchanan's inauguration in March 1857, the capital began its social season with some of the most elaborate bachelor parties of all time. The new president was wealthy, an epicurean, a bachelor with a flair for society and an impeccable knowledge of its ways. He appointed his niece, Harriet Lane, his first lady.

A lovely lady of 25, Harriet had been well trained for her new role. She attended school in Georgetown and weekends visited her uncle, who was then Secretary of State, to observe the ways of the fashionable world. After a few seasons in this society, she accompanied her Uncle James to Great Britain, where he served as U.S. minister to the Court of St. James. This training set the stage for her to assume the duties of the first lady of the White House.

White House receptions were gorgeous displays of finery. Harriet Lane's personal beauty and full figure were displayed to advantage in her hoop skirts and low bodice of Victorian fashion. Mrs. Clement Clay of Alabama described one of these scenes: "Low necks and lace berthas, made fashionable by Miss Lane, were worn almost universally, either with open sleeves revealing inner ones of filmy lace, or sleeves of the shortest form."

During these years of wonderful parties that reached a peak in 1860, the president hosted many a wide assortment of delegations. A Japanese delegation was given a state dinner which was presided over by the president and Miss Lane with members of the cabinet and a few cabinet wives and some senators. When the guests left, a whole room was required to display the gifts that included saddles, curtains, screens, swords, writing cases, and a tea set inlaid with pearls and gold.

All the right people were on his guest list. One of those included was Jefferson Davis, a friend of the president for many years. Mr. Davis was much impressed with the formal elegance of European society and compared the Buchanan parties to an "elegant republican court."

Even though the president and Jefferson Davis disagreed on the slavery issue, they remained close friends during the ensuing years. Miss Lane discovered that both had a favorite dessert, Chess Pie, and she served it often when the two dined together.

Pie Dish

A Bachelor President (cont.)

Chapter 9

Sweet Treats

Old-Fashioned Chess Pie

1 pastry shell (8 inches)

1 1/2 cups sugar

1 tablespoon plus 1 teaspoon cornmeal

1 stick (1/2 cup) butter, melted

1 tablespoon vinegar

1/2 teaspoon vanilla extract

3 eggs, beaten

Prepare pastry shell; chill 30 minutes. In a large bowl, mix sugar, cornmeal, butter, vinegar and vanilla extract. Stir in beaten eggs and mix thoroughly. Pour into pastry shell and bake at 350 degrees for 50 to 55 minutes.

Note: If you have never made chess pie, you will notice that the filling puffs as it bakes and slowly begins to fall. Very often it will crack on top. Let it cool slowly away from any drafts to minimize cracking. Regardless, it tastes just as good.

Pie Dish

INDEX

INDEX

INDEX

Notes

NOTES

Notes

NOTES

NOTES